Kingston Libraries

TD

THE ROYAL BOROUGH OF
KINGSTON
UPON THAMES

On line Services
www.kingston.gov.uk/libraries

Renew a book (5 times)
Change of address
Library news and updates
Search the catalogues

Request a book
Email a branch
Get your pin
Access free reference sites

020 8547 5006

Tudor Drive Library
Tudor Drive
Kingston upon Thames
Surrey
KT2 5QH

1 2 JUL 2019		
2 6 JUL 2019		

First published in Great Britain in 2018 by The Watts Publishing Group
Text copyright © Nicola Morgan 2018
Cover and inside design copyright © Franklin Watts 2018

10 9 8 7 6 5 4

Managing editor: Victoria Brooker
Editor: Hayley Fairhead
Cover design: Thy Bui
Inside design: Rocket Design (East Anglia) Ltd
Inside illustrations: Shutterstock

ISBN: 978 1 445 1 5814 3 (pbk)
ISBN: 978 1 445 1 5893 8 (e-book)

Printed and bound in Great Britain by Clays Ltd, Elcograf S.p.A.

Franklin Watts
An imprint of
Hachette Children's Group
Part of The Watts Publishing Group
Carmelite House
50 Victoria Embankment
London EC4Y 0DZ
An Hachette UK Company
www.hachette.co.uk
www.franklinwatts.co.uk

The website addresses (URLs) included in this book were
valid at the time of going to press. However, it is possible that
contents or addresses may have changed since the publication
of this book. No responsibility for any such changes can be
accepted by either the author or the Publisher.

For information about Nicola's books and events, and for lots of
advice and information, see www.nicolamorgan.com

★ Contents ★

A note from the author

I write a lot about adolescence and visit loads of schools. Sometimes people ask me why. Why spend so many years of my life trying to help people a quarter of my age, who are younger than my own daughters? I could just say 'Because I care' but that doesn't explain *why* I care. Why do I care more about teenagers than a load of other things I could spend my life working for? I think it has to do with my memories of being a child and teenager and how I wish I'd known the stuff I talk about now. I could have avoided a lot of stress-related illness as a young adult and felt so much better about myself if I'd understood half of what I know now.

You see, from my earliest years I was fascinated by how things work. I used to take gadgets to pieces and try to put them back together again. I wanted to know exactly how they worked, so that I could make them work better. Now, as an adult who has studied the brain and behaviour, I realise that humans and our brains are really only machines, just super-complicated and extraordinary ones. The more we know of how we work, the better we can make ourselves work. We don't know everything yet – maybe we never will – but we know a lot more than we did when I was young and that knowledge is what I want to share with you in this book.

It's for you, from me.

Introduction

Are you excited about being a teenager? Or worried? What expectations do you have: positive or negative? Parents and other adults can be very anxious about adolescence, as though they're expecting the worst. And the media often paint a negative picture, making it sound as though it's going to be *full* of stress. You might feel worried, too. This book tries to avoid that. It aims to give you all the inspiring information you need to take control of your well-being as you approach or experience this powerful and important stage of your life.

Sure, there may be some difficult days or weeks – that's life, whatever age we are. You'll have exams; friendships might cause problems; your body is changing and you may be self-conscious about that; emotions can feel out of control, making you angry or sad; and you may want to do things that parents or teachers don't want you to do, which can create conflict. But there's so much to enjoy, too!

It's exciting gaining more control over your life and growing into the person you want to be – and finding out who that is. Being able to go out more independently – with friends or on your own – is fun and helps you learn important skills for managing your own life later on. Smartphones and social media give you huge opportunities to widen your knowledge and friendships and modern technology also brings amazing chances to express yourself using video or blogging, with art, words, dance and music. Your developing brain is allowing you to become really expert in whatever skills you spend time on and you'll find that there are things you can do better than the adults around you.

Yes, you might make mistakes or a few wrong decisions along the way but that's how we learn. And adolescence is about learning: learning to become independent, to do things for yourself, have your own ideas, your own values, your own personal goals and successes. You might fail sometimes – in fact, you probably will – that's tough at the time but failure is only a step to success. If you try again, you have a better chance of succeeding and your developing brain helps that happen.

Adults worry about failure and risks and sometimes try to prevent them by sorting everything out for you. But we don't learn things or become resilient by having people do everything for us: we learn by trying it for ourselves until we manage. If we succeed through our own efforts, we feel great about it. If we succeed because our parents did it all for us or told us what to do, it's not our own achievement. And it won't feel so good.

It's really about taking control of your life and your well-being. We have to grow from being a child (when we have very little control, because we don't know enough) to being an adult (when we are supposed to have a lot of control over our own lives). Teenagers are developing the skills for this control and independence and that can't happen suddenly. *Positively Teenage* helps you learn those skills by giving you practical things you can do to have a positive impact on your well-being, mood, health and outlook. Many teenagers feel that they can't control anything: I aim to teach you that you can control far more than you think. It's what I wish I'd known when I was a teenager.

So, *Positively Teenage* is based on understanding how your brain and body work, so you can be more in control. Not just through your teenage years but through your whole life.

It will help you show adults that they can trust you, that you can learn to get things right, by aiming high and persevering. Your teenage years can be full of success if you have the right attitude, tools and knowledge. This book gives you them.

Go for it! Be positively teenage!

Well-being

You'll find the word 'well-being' everywhere these days. It's a good word because it's easy to sense what it means, because of the 'well' bit. But what does it mean *exactly*?

The best way to think about this is to see what's different about well-being compared to 'happiness'. You know what feeling happy is like. It's a positive feeling, the sort of emotion you might get if you were given a present you really wanted, or when you've done well in a test or won a race or received some praise. It's a feeling you might get during a great holiday or having fun with friends. So, we feel happy when something good happens. Sometimes we have that feeling when we don't quite know why. But we can't feel happy at the same time as feeling angry or sad, obviously. So, if we were feeling happy and then something bad happens, we stop feeling happy. Instantly.

That's where well-being is different: if you have good well-being, and something sad or bad happens, you can still have good well-being. This is because well-being is not an emotion – not an immediate feeling. Well-being is a state of physical and mental health. You build it up over time, through lots of healthy behaviours (which this book will show you) and this gives you a reserve of mental and physical health. With good well-being, you will still sometimes feel down or unwell – because everyone has those times – but you will have a general feeling of 'Yes, I'm OK; I feel pretty good a lot of the time; I can cope with what life throws at me today'.

Well-being is strongly connected to 'positive psychology'. Psychology used to focus on problems; it tried to understand how humans work, so that psychologists could help sort out our problems. But then along came positive psychology. This term was first used by Abraham Maslow, one of the world's most famous psychologists. It has become more popular with more recent scientists, such as Martin Seligman, who argued that psychology could be used to live well in the first place and make problems less likely to happen. *Positively Teenage* is a book that agrees! Positive psychology is about increasing our knowledge of how humans work and our self-understanding, so that we can have better control.

Of course, there are things in life that we can't control and some people have many more challenges than others. If lots of negative things happen, reserves of well-being can be worn away. But that makes it all the more important that we do what we can. And, luckily, most of the well-being advice is fun to follow!

FLOURISH

FLOURISH is my way of remembering all the things we need to make our brain (and body) flourish, so we can have good well-being. Our brain is not just a 1.5 kilogram lump of wet, soft stuff inside our heads – though it is that, too! It is also responsible for everything we do and think, everything we fear and love and want, and everything we are. Looking after our brain is our most important task when caring about well-being. All your thinking and feeling happens there. It's your 'control centre'. In fact, you could say that your brain *is* you: it holds your personality and a whole load of unconscious things as well as the things you choose to do.

You'll find lots of ways to incorporate **FLOURISH** into your life throughout this book. There are symbols to show you which of the **FLOURISH** elements each piece of advice is for.

HERE ARE THE EIGHT ELEMENTS OF FLOURISH

 F is for FOOD – Our brain needs fuel, just as the rest of our body does. In fact, the brain is a very fuel-hungry organ, using about 20 per cent of the energy we take in. This energy comes from food, including most liquid (but not water on its own). You won't have enough energy to make your brain and body work well if you don't have enough food. As well as having the right amount, you also need the right *sorts* of food and a good variety. Don't worry: you won't have to eat loads of foods you don't like! This is about finding things you do like.

L is for LIQUID – We need enough liquid. All drinks are made mostly of water and that water content is essential. However, some drinks are better for us than others and some are definitely not healthy.

O is for OXYGEN – Oxygen is in the air we breathe so we are obviously getting oxygen just by breathing. But some environments contain more oxygen than others and there are situations that might mean we are not getting enough to feel and function well. There are simple ways to make sure you're getting enough.

U is for USE – Different brain areas are used in different activities. The brain works on a 'use it or lose it' principle. So, if you *don't* use certain areas, you will lose connections in those areas. For example, if you learn to play the piano, you'll grow lots of connections in certain areas but if you then stop playing the piano those connections will start to weaken and disappear, though usually not completely.

R is for RELAXATION – We can't keep working all the time; if we try to, our brain soon stops working so well. Stress chemicals build up and cause problems if we don't give ourselves breaks from pressure. So, relaxation is not a luxury but an important part of well-being. When we are really busy or life is going through a challenging period, remember this especially! Don't wait until you feel you 'deserve' a break: relaxing activities will help you work better in the end.

We need to choose these activities in an informed way, though. There are suggestions later in this book.

 I is for INTEREST – Our brains work best when we are interested in what we are doing. A brain chemical called dopamine is activated when something happens to excite or interest us and this chemical helps us learn and process information. Some people call dopamine the 'pleasure chemical' and it certainly corresponds to feeling excitement and pleasure. I call it the 'yes' chemical because it makes us say, 'YES!' to things. It wakes the brain up and says, 'LOOK! This is something worth paying attention to and going for!'.

 S is for SLEEP – Scientists are discovering more and more fascinating things about sleep, including why it's so important, what it does to us and how to get the best sleep you can. We know it has a huge effect on learning, mood, stress and every aspect of well-being. Luckily, now we know lots of ways to help ourselves get the right amount of sleep. Don't worry if you have bad nights every now and then – that's quite normal, especially at times of stress or excitement – but do learn what you can do to give yourself more control over your sleep.

 H is for Happiness – Remember the difference between well-being and happiness? Well-being is more important, but having some experiences that make you feel actively *happy* is a valuable part of it. So, although there's no need to try to have every moment (or even every day) as a happy one, it's important to have *enough* things in your life that make you happy.

But what if bad things are happening to you? If you're having a bad time it becomes even more important to do some things that make you feel good, whether it's having a relaxing bath, kicking a ball about, lying in the sunshine in the park, or listening to your favourite music.

You won't achieve all the **FLOURISH** elements every day and the good news is that you don't need to! It's all about balance: you just need *enough* of each of them over a week or so. Look out for opportunities and get into the habit of thinking, 'Oh yes, I'll do that because it will help my brain in this way'. The more you can do, the better.

It's all about doing your best to make good choices – choices that will help you feel and function better, choices that will give you a positive state of well-being and the best chance of flourishing, whatever the day throws at you.

It's the key to being positively teenage.

Your *Positively Teenage* notebook

You will find a notebook useful and inspiring while you are reading *Positively Teenage*. At various points, I will suggest writing something down. There are quizzes, for example, and other things you might want to make a note of. It can be a really good way to record your progress, achievements and thoughts.

If you don't want to do this, you can just skip the bits where I suggest writing things down. If you don't have a notebook or you don't like your handwriting, you could use a computer or tablet or even your phone. It's totally up to you.

Decorate your notebook however you like. It can be neat or messy. No one else needs to see it and no one is checking your spelling!

In the future, you'll look back on your teenage years and have a record of some of your thoughts. And you'll see how much you've changed.

POSITIVE BOOST boxes

Scattered through this book you'll see boxes containing **POSITIVE BOOSTS**. If it's appropriate, it would be great to stop reading and do the suggested action right then. Or, if you can't easily do it at that moment, choose another one and do that one later. For example, if you're reading in bed before sleep and the **POSITIVE BOOST** says, 'Eat an apple' or 'Phone a friend for a chat', I am not suggesting you do it straight away!

These boosts are there for three reasons. First, to give you ideas and remind you of the possibilities; second, to make sure you do take breaks and vary your activity; and third, because they will boost your positivity and control. Build them into your life and use your imagination to invent others.

You could jot them in your notebook and add your own favourite ideas. Do one whenever you like, not just when someone tells you. It's your life.

More resources for you

You might want to find out more about some of the ideas I introduce in *Positively Teenage*. So, I've put **Resources** sections at the end of each point, with relevant websites, books and articles, so you can follow them up quickly if you're interested. My website has lots of resources for teenagers and their adults: *www.nicolamorgan.com* – and the Positively Teenage section has more specific things including some items referred to in this book: *www.nicolamorgan.com/positively-teenage/*

When I mention research, it's usually supported by a reference at the end of that point so you can investigate further. It's important to realise that there usually has to be a lot of research before we can be *sure* of something and we have to use good judgement about whether to believe particular research. I have tried to include only claims that I am as sure as possible are true and I've used the strongest science I can.

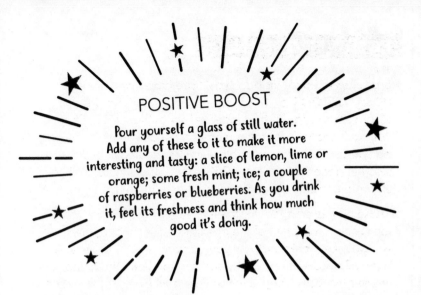

POSITIVE BOOST

Pour yourself a glass of still water.
Add any of these to it to make it more
interesting and tasty: a slice of lemon, lime or
orange; some fresh mint; ice; a couple
of raspberries or blueberries. As you drink
it, feel its freshness and think how much
good it's doing.

The FLOURISH quiz

Let's see how well you are looking after your well-being before you read this book. It's time to do the **FLOURISH** quiz! This quiz doesn't measure your well-being *exactly*, but it gives you a sense of whether you are already making good choices that will positively affect your mental and physical health. It would be a great idea to do it again when you've finished the book.

Here's what to do:

Get your notebook – or a piece of paper or laptop/tablet. (Don't write in *Positively Teenage* itself, because you'll need to do the same quiz again later.)

Look at each of the actions in the quiz and base your response on the last 24 hours. If this has been a really unusual day, that doesn't matter, but it's worth bearing in mind when you look at your score.

Score *one point* for each of these actions that you have done in the last 24 hours. Just one point, even if you did the thing twice.

Then add up the points to get your score. You'll see what each score means afterwards.

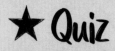 # ★ Quiz

The FLOURISH actions

 I spent at least half an hour doing something deliberately to relax.

 I kept trying at something I found difficult.

 I felt happy at some point in the day.

 I created something (writing, a dance, arts, craft, woodwork etc).

 I took part in playing music or I listened to music (properly listening, not just having it on in the background).

 I exercised so I was out of breath (or went for a walk for at least 30 minutes).

 I spent half an hour reading for pleasure. (This can be *anything* as long as it's something you want to read for pleasure, not because you have to. Reading on social media platforms or online forums doesn't count, but you can read on an e-book reader if you like. If you really don't enjoy reading, you could spend this half-hour drawing or doing a puzzle.)

 I turned my digital devices off for at least an hour before bed and didn't switch them on until I got up in the morning.

★ I spent some time engaged in a hobby.

★ I did something kind for someone else.

★ I was engaged in something so much that I forgot the time.

★ I had at least eight hours sleep.

★ I drank six glasses/cups of liquid. (Ideally, this should be water, but you may include some fruit/herbal teas, diluted juice, milk or one glass of fresh fruit juice. A cup of coffee or ordinary tea counts as a half cup. Do not include fizzy drinks or very sugary drinks, and obviously no alcohol.)

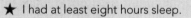

★ I ate at least five portions of the following foods: fish, chicken, beans (including soya beans), lentils, nuts, oats, eggs, dairy products (e.g. yogurt or milk), seedy or wholegrain bread, any vegetables including salad, hummus.

Your results:

12–14 Brilliant! You are caring for your brain *really* well.

9–11 Well done – you are helping your brain.

6–8 You are doing some good things for your brain – but you could make it even better.

3–5 Time to take control! Some quite simple changes will make a big difference.

0–2 Action needed! You only have one brain, and there's only one person who can look after it: you!

Try to score at least 11 every day. Don't beat yourself up if you don't always manage it – it's a target, that's all, but the more times you manage it, the better. And well done if you do!

Once you've read this book, you'll be better equipped to have a great score and to maintain that throughout your teenage years and beyond. It's the foundation of being positively teenage. The rest of the book will help you do this easily.

Positively You

We are all the same because we are all human. But we are also all different from each other: each of us is literally unique. So, how does this work and what does it mean? And what has understanding this got to do with well-being?

I'll answer that last question first because it's quite simple: understanding ourselves is the beginning of being able to control our lives. The ancient Greeks had a motto: 'Know Yourself', and this is exactly what I mean. First, we need to know what humans are like, how we operate and feel, the basics of human psychology and behaviour. If we know that, we can understand the idea that: *I am behaving like this because this is how humans behave; it's normal.*

Second, we need to know how we *each* behave – the ways in which we are different from other people. If we know that, we can understand the idea that: *I feel this or do this because I am this sort of person; this is part of me; I might be able to change some behaviours if I want to, but this is who I am.*

Let's look at what makes us the same

A human is a species of animal. Humans share certain things: how our brains and bodies work, how we grow and develop, what we are capable of. If you think of other animals – cats or dolphins or eagles, for example – you'll be able to think of certain things or behaviours that make them cats, dolphins or eagles, things they each have or do that the others don't. Cats, humans and dolphins share some characteristics – for example, they all breathe and they are all mammals – but we can identify a cat, human or dolphin from each other. And even though there are lots of different sorts of cats, many of which look very different, we know they are cats because of their long tails, fur, whiskers, paws, ear-shape etc.

Perhaps the most important thing that makes humans stand out as different and 'human' is the size of our brain and some of the powerful things we can do with it. One part of our brain is particularly large compared with other animals: the prefrontal cortex. If you touch your forehead, your prefrontal cortex is right there behind your skull.

The prefrontal cortex is often called the control centre and we certainly need it when we want control over actions, words and decisions. But it's more than that. It's what we use for thinking about anything: working things out, for example, or looking ahead to what might happen, using our knowledge and understanding.

So, the power of our prefrontal cortex is one of the most important features of being human. It's one way in which we are the same as each other, wherever in the world we live, whatever colour, gender or age we are or whatever religious beliefs we have; whether we're poor or rich, at peace or war, bully or victim, sick or healthy, kind or cruel, artist, athlete, nurse, scientist, teacher, shop worker, builder or politician. We are all the same: human, with a human prefrontal cortex, human powers, human behaviours and human emotions. We all bleed; we all hurt. We should never forget that.

But we are also all individual. There are no two people in the world who are *exactly* the same. Even identical twins, who began from the same egg and share identical genes, are not the exact same people, though they may be *very* similar. If you look at the things that can make us turn out different, you'll see that some of them apply to identical twins, too.

Let's look at what makes us different

Different genes we inherited from our biological parents: 'inherit' means to take from a previous generation. We inherit genes from our parents, some from our biological mother and some from our biological father. If you have an older or younger sibling, they will inherit a different combination of genes, so you might have some things that are the same and some that are different. If you have an identical sibling, your genes will be identical because you came from the same egg, fertilised by the same sperm.

Everything that has happened to us since the moment we were born: from huge life events, such as bereavement or illness, to smaller things, such as hearing someone say something kind or cruel, being ignored or praised. (It's possible that things that happened while we were in our mother's womb might have made a difference, too, though we can't be sure what those differences are and scientific understanding is still growing about this.)

The values and ideas we learn from people around us: when we are children, we tend to absorb and agree with the views we hear from adults around us. So, if you are brought up with parents who hold particular opinions, you will probably share those views at first. As you go through adolescence, you may start to develop your own and they may be different in small or large ways.

The things we have spent time doing: each of us has spent different amounts of time on different activities. Some have learnt a musical instrument or played badminton; some spend loads of time climbing trees or riding horses or singing or acting or doing maths puzzles or reading books. Everything we spend time on alters us a bit, changing our brain, our knowledge, skills and tastes.

Our age and stage of life: at different stages of life we will have different skills and knowledge and different desires, responsibilities, needs and priorities. A teenager has different things to think about from a small child who relies on their parents for everything; a new parent has different concerns from someone the same age but without children; someone in their thirties will have different concerns from someone just retiring.

Those are the *causes* of our differences but what exactly *are* our differences? Let's look at some of the important ways in which you might be different from some other people. What makes you individual and unique? This is what you need to know, if you are to 'Know Yourself' and be positively you.

POSITIVE BOOST

Make a poster of an inspirational quote that you like. You can find loads online by searching 'inspirational quotes'. There are also lots of greetings cards that would work if you don't fancy making something yourself. Choose one that reflects something you can believe in, something to hold onto and live your life by. Making a poster for your room will keep reminding you of the positive message.

Your teenage brain

Until the late 1990s, we didn't even know there was anything special about the teenage brain! Scientists thought it was just a bit more developed than a younger brain and a bit less developed than an adult brain. Now we know about fascinating changes that can help explain a lot of common teenage experiences.

It can be incredibly reassuring and empowering to understand that the changes that you might experience and the feelings you might have are completely normal and that many of them have a biological cause. If you do experience some of the more negative things I'm about to mention, try not to worry or blame yourself. Yes, you can certainly try to overcome them – and the more you try the sooner you're likely to succeed – but these challenges are not your *fault*: there are some biological causes, in the form of hormone and brain changes, as well as more social causes, such as needing to fit in with your peers or dealing with routine pressures. Also, remember that this stage doesn't last forever. Whatever feelings or experiences you are going through are only temporary. That sounds obvious but it's easy to forget.

The main things to know about teenage brain changes

This is not just a human thing: adolescent rats and monkeys (and maybe other mammals, too) have some similar brain changes and behaviours during puberty.

It's not modern: authors have written in negative ways about adolescents for hundreds of years. Shakespeare, for example, refers negatively to your age group several times, listing various behaviours that sound like today's negative stereotypes. He even puts an age range on it: ten to 23 – and it turns out he was not far wrong! We know now that teenage brain changes start at around about 11 (often a bit earlier, especially for girls) and don't finish until well into your twenties.

There are three stages of change: first, you grow many more connections between neurons (nerve cells, which carry messages around the brain and down the spinal cord). The peak age for this is around 11 for girls and 12 for boys (on average). Next, you lose lots of connections. That sounds worrying but it's completely natural and it's a very important stage. Think of it as a bit like pruning a tree: if a gardener cuts back all the weak and straggly branches the tree will be stronger. Finally, starting at roughly 15 or 16, the remaining connections become stronger. They become covered with a substance called myelin which coats the connections and makes them better at sending messages.

The last brain area to become fully developed is the prefrontal cortex: I mentioned this earlier and described it as the 'control centre', but you might like to know a few special things this brain area is for:

✱ Controlling impulses and temptations

✱ Understanding emotions and controlling responses to them

✱ Understanding what someone else is feeling

✳ Judging whether something is a sensible or risky thing to do and making the right decision about it

✳ Predicting the results of actions.

A set of areas that *is* very well developed in teenagers is the limbic system, including the amygdala. This system is responsible for:

✳ Emotions – including anger, sadness and fear

✳ Stress responses – 'fight or flight'

✳ Instinctive reactions

✳ Impulse, temptation and desire to do something

✳ Pleasure and reward.

Teenagers have more brain activity than adults in brain areas that are active during embarrassment (during situations that are socially embarrassing, such as making a mistake in front of your friends). Adults often notice that teenagers can seem super-embarrassed by something an adult wouldn't really bother about. Well, it may be that you really *are* feeling more embarrassed.

Sleep patterns change:

1. You need more sleep than adults: about nine-and-a-quarter hours a night on average, compared to eight hours for adults. (These are averages and some people manage very well on less, while others seem to need more.)

2. Your 'sleep hormone', melatonin, doesn't switch on until late at night, similar to adults, so it's not easy to fall asleep early.

3. Worse still, your melatonin levels don't switch *off* early in the morning, so you're likely to be sleepy at school.

Luckily, there are lots of things you can do to get more sleep. After all, this wouldn't be *Positively Teenage* if I weren't going to give you lots of positive strategies! That comes under **Sleep well** in the POSITIVELY HEALTHY section on page 110.

★ Quiz

Let's take a look at how many teenage changes you're aware of in yourself. All these are 'normal' things to experience but it's also normal not to experience all of them. People reach each stage in their own time and differently. Write all these things in your notebook. Tick the ones you've noticed in yourself and write a comment or example if you want to. (You'll find another version of this quiz on the positively teenage section of my website. It's completely anonymous and I'd love you to fill it in, as it aids my research and helps me to help you!)

★ Feeling irritable and snappy

★ Feeling that parents and adults are not really on my side

★ Having more arguments with my parents than I used to

★ Not being able to wake up easily in the morning

★ Not being able to get to sleep at night

★ Feeling sad or anxious much more than I used to

★ Being really self-conscious and embarrassed that people are looking at me

★ Doing things I know are not sensible, because my friends are doing them

★ Thinking and daydreaming about boys or girls I'm attracted to a *lot*

★ Often wishing I could solve big problems in the world.

Then write down any other things you find noticeable about being the age you are. What are you feeling? What upsets or worries you? Or do you love everything or most things about the age you are?

Based on that, what do you think are your big teenage issues? Would you like to see if your friends would do the quiz?

Resources

TEENAGE BRAINS

My book aimed directly at young people:
Blame My Brain – The Amazing Teenage Brain Revealed

Two sites with lots of references to the science behind teenage brain differences: *www.pbs.org/wgbh/pages/frontline/shows/teenbrain/*
and *teenmentalhealth.org/learn/the-teen-brain-2/*

Shakespeare's comment from *The Winter's Tale*, Act III Scene 3:

'I would there were no age between ten and three and twenty, or that youth would sleep out the rest; for there is nothing in the between but getting wenches with child, wronging the anciency, stealing, fighting…'

National Sleep Foundation webpages for teenagers: *sleepfoundation. org/sleep-topics/teens-and-sleep*

Research on the impact of smart phones on children's sleeping patterns: *jamanetwork.com/journals/jamapediatrics/article-abstract/2571467*

Research on how rats' sleeping patterns change with age: *www.journalsleep.org/Articles/220202.pdf*

Your teenage body

So, what else makes teenagers different? Our bodies change throughout our life. Your body will change a lot between the age of ten and the end of adolescence. You've almost certainly learnt about this at school, from your parents and from magazines. Also, depending on your age, you'll have noticed changes yourself.

This isn't a book about puberty so I'm not going to go into the details. I've put some websites on page 29 that will answer any questions you might have about something you've noticed happening to your body. What I want to do is help you have a positive attitude to your body as it changes.

There are three things to remember. Reminding yourself of these facts will help you hugely.

1. Everyone is different.

2. What you see on the Internet and in magazines is usually faked.

3. Most people have something they don't like about their bodies.

Let's explore these three points now.

1. Everyone is different. Some bodies change a lot and quickly; others don't change so much and do it slowly. Try not to compare yourself to the people around you, although I know this can be difficult. What your body is doing says nothing about the person you are.

Some people are excited and positive about their body changes. It's easier to feel like this if you are developing at the same rate as most of your friends – an 'average' rate. But if you are developing earlier than your friends, you might feel more self-conscious or negative about it. You might even try to hide your changes so people don't notice. Please don't feel you have to do this: it's going to be such a short time before your friends catch up. Just be proud of leading the way!

Or you might be developing later, and that can be upsetting, too, as you probably want to be just like your friends. Both boys and girls can be embarrassed by not developing the outward signs of physical maturity. But some teenagers just do develop more slowly or later than others. It's not a race or a competition: it's just that everyone's bodies are naturally different. It is very rare for this to be caused by a medical problem but, if you are worried, it's worth seeing a doctor for reassurance (or investigation if you are one of those rare cases).

Of course, those questioning or uncomfortable with their gender may well have extra difficulties here. Now would be the time to get expert advice if you haven't already. See the **Resources** panel on page 29.

2. What you see on the Internet and in magazines is usually faked. Photos and videos showing models and actors (and even vloggers and other video-makers) are almost always 'enhanced' and 'perfected' in some way. Even your friends' photos on social media have usually been selected as the ONE photo out of dozens or hundreds of selfies that they didn't like.

If you don't keep reminding yourself of this, it can be a real cause of low self-esteem. To be honest, it's better to look at those pictures and videos as little as possible. Or, if you do look, remind yourself (often) that the person looks that way because of professional make-up that has taken ages; clever lighting; and photo-enhancing software to airbrush out wrinkles or rolls or curves and often to make someone look far thinner than they really are.

When those people don't have those advantages, or they've just woken up in the morning, they are just like everyone else.

3. Most people, especially in wealthier societies with a big culture of advertising, have something they don't like about their bodies. Even the people you think have a fantastic body/face/hair/whatever. This is the saddest thing about the whole issue: too many people are going around dissatisfied with something trivial about their physical appearance. A fortune is spent on breast enhancements or reductions, nose-straightening or nose-reducing, whitening teeth or changing the colour of skin.

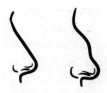

Let me tell you something I only remembered as I was writing this: I used to hate my nose. I thought it was way too big. I didn't do anything about it, thank goodness, but at some point it became such a non-issue that I had literally forgotten about it until now. I looked in the mirror after writing that, just to check, and found myself thinking, 'Really? What was all that about?'

Does this mean we should just ignore our bodies and faces and not look after them? No, I don't think so. There are natural and important ways to have strong, healthy bodies, face, skin and hair, which I'll come to in POSITIVELY HEALTHY on page 74. It's right to take care of those things and it's completely fine if we want to emphasise the bits we prefer and downplay the bits we don't like. We might use hair-styling, choose certain clothes, use a few products that might help. But we need to keep it in perspective. Too much effort, worry or money spent on changing how we look is only going to lead to more unhappiness and stop us focusing on important ways to make the most out of life. Focusing on negatives stops us enjoying or even noticing the positives and that's a real shame.

Of course, if you have a condition which affects your appearance or something noticeable which is causing you major problems in your life, it's understandable that you might want a medical solution if there is one. If you have something like this and it's upsetting you, do talk to a doctor and say how you feel.

But when I talk about being unhappy about your appearance, I'm talking about the range of natural body changes that happen during adolescence. I want to encourage you to feel either good or at least OK about them, however quickly or slowly they are happening.

We are all different; no one is as perfect as a professional photo; and there are more important things to think about than whether our breasts or nose or muscles or size or voice or hair are 'perfect'. If you look for perfection, you'll never find it but you'll spoil your life by trying. And what is perfection anyway?

You are you; you are changing all the time; how your body is now is not how it will be next month or next year. Just be healthy and try to forget the rest or at least let it occupy the smallest amount of your brain-space possible.

You'll find lots of tips about living healthily and looking after your body in POSITIVELY HEALTHY on page 74.

Resources

For masses of information on teenage health and well-being:

Agnes – the life guide for girls. I think this is an awesome site and I wish I could find something similar for boys: *agnesforgirls.com/*

Health for Teens: *www.healthforteens.co.uk*

Kids Health: *kidshealth.org/en/teens*

TEENAGE BODY CHANGES

Aimed at girls: *www.girlshealth.gov/body/index.html*
Aimed at boys: *www.youngmenshealthsite.org*
For all: *http://www.nhs.uk/Livewell/puberty/Pages/puberty-signs.aspx*

BODY IMAGE

Media Smart has a brilliant resource aimed at boys, but also useful for girls: *mediasmart.uk.com/resources/teaching-resources/body-image-1*

And there's a useful YouTube video here, with a similar message: *www.youtube.com/watch?v=24Xa1Nw8eJY*

PBS on raising a girl with a positive body image: *www.pbs.org/parents/parenting/raising-girls/body-image-identity/ raising-a-girl-with-a-positive-body-image/*

Kids Health for teenagers: *kidshealth.org/en/teens/body-image.html*

Kids Health for parents: *kidshealth.org/en/parents/body-image.html*

Family Life, for parents: *www.familylives.org.uk/advice/teenagers/ health-well-being/body-image/*

GENDER IDENTITY QUESTIONS

In the UK, Young Stonewall has advice: *www.youngstonewall.org.uk/ lgbtq-info/gender-identity*.

There's also Mermaids: *www.mermaidsuk.org.uk/*

Know and value your 'character strengths'

Schools tend to focus on measuring skills that are an obvious part of the curriculum, particularly subjects with exams as the goal. I don't blame schools: it's what they have to do.

But we need many other abilities in order to do well in life. Some of these are called 'character strengths' and are important for well-being. They also affect performance and success, partly because well-being helps success, but also because the strengths include things like 'perseverance', which obviously affect your work. There are ways to measure these strengths, as you'll see. Each person has different character strengths.

The particular strengths I'll refer to are the 24 character strengths listed by the VIA Institute on Character. They have been well researched: over five million people have taken the survey and there's masses of information on their website (see page 35) which will allow you to find out more.

Here are the 24 character strengths in alphabetical order. With permission from the VIA Institute, I have adapted the descriptions for this book, adding in questions to help you think about the meanings of each one.

Appreciation of Beauty and Excellence – do you get a buzz from seeing something you think is beautiful? Do you feel admiration when you see something that required real skill?

Bravery – how willing are you to try things you might fail at? Do you try out for teams even though you might not be selected or might not excel? Do you stand up for your opinions even if others disagree?

Creativity – do you spend time on art, music, photography, writing, or a hobby involving making things? Do you have creative ideas and imagination? Do you tend to have unusual approaches to problems?

Curiosity – are you keen to investigate and discover new things? Do you like new experiences? Do you want to know how things work?

Fairness – how important are fairness and justice to you? Do you feel angry when you see someone being treated unfairly or when you have been treated unfairly? If there was a rule you thought was unfair, would you fight to have it changed?

Forgiveness – can you 'move on' after someone has apologised (or even if they haven't)? Or do you hold grudges and think differently of the person who has wronged you, even after the incident has blown over?

Gratitude – do you feel and show gratitude for good things in your life? Are you aware of the good things and are you able to remember them when something bad happens?

Honesty – are you true to yourself, not pretending to be who you aren't? Do you value sincerity, truthfulness and honesty?

Hope – how optimistic are you about life? Do you expect good things to happen to you? If you imagine your future, is it bright? Do you describe yourself as a mostly lucky person?

Humility – when you've achieved something excellent, are you able not to boast about it? Are you a modest person, able to praise other people's achievements?

Humour – are you often playful and light-hearted? Do you tend to see the lighter side of a situation and find humour even when things are difficult?

Judgement – are you good at critical thinking – thinking through all sides of an argument and not jumping to conclusions?

Kindness – do you enjoy doing things for others? Do you make sacrifices for other people?

Leadership – are you keen on organising other people to get things done? Do you find you can positively influence others to get them to work towards a goal?

Love – are you able to love and to accept when someone loves you? Is it important to you to be close to others and to genuinely like them?

Love of Learning – do you like practising and becoming expert at new skills and topics, adding to your knowledge? Do you enjoy learning new facts and understanding more?

Perspective (you might also call this wisdom) – do you often manage to come to a sensible and logical conclusion about things rather than acting on emotion? Can you think about and discuss moral issues and see other people's points of view, so that you can find a solution that isn't just about what you want?

Perseverance – if you don't succeed the first time, are you strong and resilient enough to try again? Can you think of something you kept trying at even though it didn't work out several times?

Prudence – are you careful and thoughtful about your choices and actions? Are you able to be cautious when necessary and avoid too much risk?

Self-regulation – do you have good self-control, being able to stop yourself doing something that is tempting? When you know there's something you shouldn't do, are you able to stop yourself? When you feel angry, are you able to control this well?

Social intelligence (you might call this empathy) – how in tune are you with others? Do you care what others are feeling? Do you often try to help when someone is feeling bad? How aware are you that different people may think and feel things differently from you?

Spirituality – do you have a spiritual side? Do you have faith in a higher meaning or a religion that you feel connected to and that gives you comfort?

Teamwork – is it important to you to work well in a team? Do you think society needs people like you who are socially responsible and think of others? Are you a loyal person and do you value supporting other people? Would you call yourself a good citizen in your family, your school, your groups or the wider community?

Zest – how much energy do you usually feel? Do you approach most activities in a positive, excited way? If you're about to try something new or tackle a problem, do you dive in with enthusiasm and a 'can do' approach?

★ Assess your character strengths

The only way to get an accurate picture of your character strengths is to do the survey on the VIA website. But if you can't do that now or prefer not to, here are ways to think about these strengths in relation to you. You could also do this activity and *then* do the actual survey and see whether you were right! Use your *Positively Teenage* notebook, or whatever you've been using, to record your answers.

 Write down the four or five strengths you *believe* you would score best on.

 Write down the three to five strengths you believe you would score least well on.

★ Can you think of one or two reasons or examples for why you chose each one?

 For your strongest ones, can you think of one action you could perform in the next few days that would build it further?

★ For your weakest ones, think about whether you would like to improve these strengths. If there is one that you really don't care about, cross it out. For each of the strengths, can you think of one action you could perform in the next few days that would improve it?

Write them as goals: things you plan to do. Make your goals clear, achievable and easy to measure. (You might want to look at **Set the right goals** in A POSITIVE ATTITUDE on page 60.)

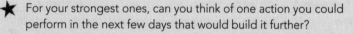

You can build a positive attitude and grow your self-esteem if you find ways to exercise your main strengths even more *and* do simple things to boost your lesser ones. These are not fixed skills: you can improve them if you want to. Just keep them in mind and look out for opportunities. (You'll also find a use for them in **Notice what went well** in A POSITIVE ATTITUDE on page 70.)

POSITIVE BOOST

Write a thank you note or card to someone who has done something kind to you or whose support you appreciate. It could just be a text message or it could be a home-made card to your sister or dad or teacher or friend. You'll feel good and so will they – double win!

Resources

CHARACTER STRENGTHS

For the free survey which lets you measure your character strengths: www.viacharacter.org/www/Character-Strengths/VIA-Classification
Look for the VIA Youth survey for people aged 10–17. (Note that you have to register your email address, so check with an adult about whether you are allowed to do this.)

For research into the role of character strengths: www.viacharacter.org/www/Research/Character-Research-Findings

(The character strengths are © Copyright 2004–2018, VIA Institute on Character. All rights reserved. Used with permission. www.viacharacter.org)

Your different personality

→ and the need for quiet

Another thing that makes us each different is our personality. Some people are anxious and easily stressed; some are really ambitious, while others are more content with smaller goals; some are leaders and others have no desire to lead; some like working in teams and others prefer to do things on their own. People differ in how selfish, vain, optimistic or patient they are.

It's good to acknowledge personality differences and try not to compare ourselves with someone else. Of course, there are some behaviours we might like to change – doing selfish things, for example, is not something to be proud of. But there's no such thing as a perfect personality and a positive approach is to say to yourself: 'If I behave in a way I don't like, I can change that behaviour, though it might be difficult. I can change negative behaviours while still keeping my personality.'

There is one personality difference that seriously affects well-being. I won't suggest you change it – you probably can't. But if you understand it, you can take steps to approach it positively. Let's look at introversion and extroversion.

Introvert or extrovert?

You might think introversion is about shyness and extroversion is about liveliness. They're not. Introverts and extroverts can both be shy or lively. It's about how our bodies and brains react to social situations and how we spend or gain energy from those situations.

Social situations are everything from a super-relaxed chat with your best friend to walking into a crowded dining-hall where you don't know anyone. They include collaborative work, making a speech and answering questions in class. Anything where you interact directly with people.

Introverts

Introverts usually react more strongly in social situations, often feeling more stressed and becoming more tired. They can handle them perfectly well (though they may need to practise and get used to the situation) and, in fact, introverts can be brilliant at public-speaking and making conversation because they are very sensitive to the audience and work hard to please. But introverts will use more energy to cope and therefore be more tired after these situations.

School is FULL of such situations! In fact, the only time when you're not in a social situation during a school day is when you're working on a piece of work on your own. The rest of the time, as an introvert you're spending energy and becoming exhausted dealing with a barrage of social situations. That's not good for your well-being and performance.

Extroverts

Similarly, if you are more of an extrovert, you *need* these social situations, otherwise you may get bored, frustrated,

POSITIVELY YOU

A POSITIVE ATTITUDE

POSITIVELY HEALTHY

POSITIVELY BRAINY

POSITIVE ABOUT PEOPLE

A POSITIVE MOOD

uninterested or disengaged. Extroverts feel energised after social interaction and thrive on being around other people. You'll get enough of it during a school day but you may need to seek social activities at weekends.

★ The introvert/extrovert quiz

You might want to know where you are on the introvert/extrovert scale, though you may already have a good idea. There are free quizzes online (with links on the *Positively Teenage* website) but here are six statements for now. The more strongly you agree with them, the more likely you are to be towards the introverted end of the scale:

★ I often think, 'I really need to be on my own for a bit'.

★ I get tired after talking to friends for a long time and I feel better after a break.

★ I like chatting to just a couple of friends more than being with a larger group.

★ I really prefer quiet places to noisy, lively ones.

★ I find my mind becomes overloaded when I'm with other people and the noise can be stressful. I often make excuses to leave

★ I much prefer working on my own to doing shared work.

Positive strategies to work with your introvert or extrovert needs

Accept and value your personality, however introvert or extrovert you are. Each trait has advantages and they are each equally valuable. Remembering that most people are a bit of a mixture, here are some different possible advantages:

* Both can be great friends: introverts listen well and are sensitive to the needs of others; extroverts can raise the mood of the people round them and inject fun into a group.

* Both can be really good public speakers: introverts are likely to think carefully about what the audience wants and respond to feedback; extroverts tend to be less self-conscious and bring a natural energy to a performance, often finding it easy to make people laugh.

* Both can be excellent leaders: introverts can make the rest of the team feel listened to and respected; extroverts may carry difficult ideas or decisions through more easily.

* Both can be equally creative: introverts tend to come up with their best ideas alone, while extroverts do so better in a group.

Encourage your teachers to investigate and understand these personality traits because they are bound to have both introverts and extroverts in every classroom and different activities suit different learners. Point them towards the **Resources** on page 41. Some teachers may need to adapt their teaching style to work equally well with both personality types. So much school work is collaborative nowadays, and teachers need to be attuned to ways to make this work equally well for everyone and not assume that everyone loves working in pairs or groups.

If you are quite introverted, think of ways to get enough peace and quiet to feel refreshed and ready to work. It's important not to run away from social interaction but you need enough quiet time. Talk to your school librarian, as the library can often be a good place for sanctuary and time out. Every school should provide a place, time and permission to chill out – where people are not required to be social when they don't want to be.

Whether you're more extrovert or introvert, be clear about your needs. If you want time out during break or lunch, or at weekends, explain to friends that you are absolutely fine but you just want a bit of time to regain your energy or do some thinking. Make sure people realise you are genuinely fine, so they don't come and bother you. When you get home from school, if you want to be alone for a bit, say so.

Similarly, if you're pretty extrovert and you're desperate for more social stuff, look for others who'd like to get together, have a spontaneous party, picnic or cinema trip at the weekend, join a drama group or any other group-based activity. Just tell people openly that you're someone who needs lots of social activity but you understand that not everyone does.

Share this knowledge about introversion and extroversion with your friends. Many of them will be really pleased to understand themselves better, too! You could all have some fun doing an online quiz to 'measure' your introversion/extroversion and start to value each other's skills.

Be brave and tackle things you find difficult. Extroverts need to learn to be on their own sometimes and introverts need to learn to be social and perform in front of others. Those are skills we need in life and they make us feel good. So, don't run away from them. Whatever you need help with, ask for it. Usually, whatever we are trying to do, it's easier to take small steps and get used to difficult things gradually.

POSITIVE BOOST

Make a sign to go on your bedroom door that tells your family whether you want to be alone. Use a positive message, such as: 'Thinker at work – peace needed' or 'I love you all but this is me-time' or 'Silent zone – I'm working' or whatever is appropriate. Explain to your family that when this sign is there, they should respect it.

Celebrate your personality with a t-shirt or a mug! There are products you can buy that have amusing and inspiring quotes about this. By doing this, you'll be making a statement and sharing useful knowledge.

Resources

INTROVERSION AND EXTROVERSION

A book aimed at young people, parents and schools, especially focusing on being an introvert in school: *Quiet Power* by Susan Cain

The Quiet Revolution website, with advice and stories for introverts and extroverts on how to appreciate our quiet sides: *www.quietrev.com/*

A nice interview with Susan Cain, aimed at parents of introverted teenagers, but I think interesting for young people, too: *http://yourteenmag.com/family-life/communication/susan-cain-introverted-teenager*

A detailed look at what it means to be introverted or extroverted: *http://www.thedebrief.co.uk/news/opinion/introvert-extrovert-what-does-it-mean-20160463230*

An article on being a sensitive extrovert: *www.psychologytoday.com/blog/sense-and-sensitivity/201408/how-cope-highly-sensitive-extrovert*
It's a small piece but quite useful because it avoids the trap of thinking that it's all about shyness: yes, you can be extrovert and sensitive.

FEELING SHY
A couple of reassuring looks at shyness and social phobia:

Moodjuice: *www.moodjuice.scot.nhs.uk/shynesssocialphobia.asp*

Kids Health: *http://kidshealth.org/en/teens/shy-tips.html*

Different lives

Different people experience easier or harder situations. I don't think anyone can go through life without any hurdles. Would you want that? I wouldn't. I'd feel uncomfortable to be so lucky! And it *would* be luck, too. The things that make us proud are when we manage to overcome hurdles and challenges. They may have been tough at the time, but looking back we can be proud of how we coped.

Some challenges are huge, more than we can manage on our own. Some seem big at first but turn out to be more manageable than expected. Often, worrying is worse than the actual problem. Other situations are more minor. Some are temporary and others permanent.

I don't want to focus too much on these problems – this is a book about positives, not negatives – but I think we should remember that everyone has something going on and that it affects how easy it is to develop well-being. It won't make it impossible – you can have good well-being even when bad things happen – but it makes a difference. And acknowledging this is a positive start. If you are going through bad stuff, don't be too hard on yourself. Ask for help when you need it and go easy on yourself.

Things that make lives different

Money – for many families, money is a big worry. Money problems can affect the health and well-being of the adults you live with and also impact on your own life.

Family – every family is different. Try not to compare yourself with others, because you only know your own family properly – others can seem perfect when they aren't. There's no rule that says what sort of family works best, either. So whether you have one parent, or two, or more, whether you have siblings or not, none of that predicts how well your family will work.

Illness – either for you or someone you love. This includes mental illness, of course.

Disability – a whole range of possible challenges.

Gender – if you are uncomfortable with or questioning the gender you've been brought up with, or being pushed in one direction or another by people around you, this will make your preoccupations different from someone who isn't thinking about these things.

Sexuality – at some point, you will probably find yourself attracted sexually towards someone. This could be simple or complicated, depending on who you're attracted to and the reactions of people around you.

Religion and culture – during adolescence you might start questioning whichever religion or culture you've been brought up in. Also, the cultural and religious rules you follow may be different from those of your friends.

Random events – your family could go through any number of difficult events. Even relatively ordinary things like moving house or moving school can change things for you and your family.

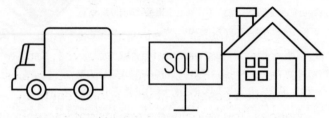

Childhood history – some people have a difficult start in life. There are various reasons why this can happen. Being a parent is not easy and some parents struggle more than others.

There are loads of smaller things, too. If you think about it, every family is made up of individuals with different personalities. So, every family and every home is different. You have the one you've got, until you leave and make your own home. Then you can do things differently or the same – it will be up to you!

Summing up

You've seen lots of ways in which you are individual – features that make you, you. You've discovered special differences in teenage brains and looked positively at your adolescent body changes. You've gained a real insight into your own valuable character strengths and thought about ways to develop the ones you want to. Your introvert and extrovert features make more sense to you now and you've seen how to value your individual personality.

Thinking about some of the many possible differences between people's lives has helped you see yourself in context, too. Understanding and recognising all these human differences will help as you navigate your adolescence. You are on your way to being able to tackle any challenges positively and sail strongly through these years.

Now let's look at making the most of those differences and creating some real routes to lifelong success.

A Positive Attitude

Looking after ourselves begins with the right attitude. Otherwise, we won't bother to try. This section takes a look at some ways of thinking which will make a positive difference to your life now, through adolescence and beyond. There's a way I'd like you to think about this.

First, what is 'a thought'? It feels like a vague, invisible idea that floats through your head. It doesn't feel like a physical thing. But a thought is a physical thing. It's the result of an electrical signal passing through some pathways between the neurons in your brain, often at huge speed. (The speed varies, depending on things like which networks are involved, but 150 metres per second would be quite usual.)

Next, realise that each time you have the same thought it uses the same network of pathways between the neurons.

Now understand that each time you use that network, you make those pathways stronger. You know how, if you walk through snow, and then you walk along the same route several times, you will make that path more obvious, stronger and easier to follow each time? That's what happens in your brain when you think or do the same thing lots of times.

I'll talk about this again when I talk about the power of practising. But, for the moment, just think about the fact that each time you have the same thought, you make it easier to have that thought again because you make the pathways stronger. (On the *Positively Teenage* page of my website, you'll find a link to a neat presentation that demonstrates this idea of pathways.)

Your thought could be a positive one or a negative one. It could be: 'I did well in that test' or 'I'm bad at science'. It could be: 'If I work hard I can pass that test' or 'I'm not as clever as the rest of my class'. It could be: 'I'm really glad I met Lucy' or 'People don't like me'. By having that thought, you make it more likely you'll have it again. And if you think it over and over again, you make a physical path in your brain that allows that thought to keep coming.

Finally, realise that this means that if you have negative thoughts, over and over again, you are creating physical pathways in your brain – pathways of negative thinking.

Have you heard of 'brainwashing'? You might have read a book where someone is 'brainwashed'. It sometimes comes into science-fiction or thrillers, where villains change the thoughts of victims so they think the way the villains want. Brainwashing happens: it's what we do to ourselves every time we keep having repeated thoughts, whether positive or negative. And you have more control over that than you think.

This is why people so often talk about the need to think positive thoughts. And it's why athletes and other performers are encouraged to imagine or picture themselves succeeding. Imagining is just the same as thinking: it makes a pathway in our brain.

Focus on what you can control

A positive attitude begins with being able to focus on what we can control and ignore what we can't. It's sometimes very difficult to do and I admit, I often struggle! But being able to do this as much as possible is a crucial part of well-being.

Do you often worry about: things you can't control; things that probably won't happen; things that have already happened and that it's way too late to change; events happening in the news; things about your appearance that you don't like? Do thoughts like this sometimes keep you awake at night? Or stop you concentrating on things you're supposed to be concentrating on? Welcome to the world of the worrier!

It's quite natural but it's not pleasant or useful. In fact, it's sometimes the opposite of useful because it takes away time from the things you *could* usefully think about. There are things worth worrying about but they should be the right things at the right time.

But what are they and how do we do that?

Let's break it down into types of worry and think about whether they are worth spending time on. (Of course, if something bad has happened, it's normal and healthy to feel negative for a certain amount of time, but I'm talking about spending *time* thinking about the wrong worries.) Do you spend your time thinking about…

…things that have already happened, which you had no control over? (For example, you didn't get picked for the team or school play because, even though you did your best, someone else was better, or you were ill and couldn't do your best.)

→ *Totally out of your control: try not to dwell on these worries. Of course, it's normal to feel upset, but stop thinking about it as soon as you can. Look ahead to the next chance.*

…things that have happened, which might have happened differently if you'd done something different? (For example, not doing as well as you should in a test.)

$$\frac{4}{10}$$

→ *You can't change the past but you can work out if there was something you could do differently next time. Once you've worked that out, move on.*

…things which have happened, so you can't change them, but there's something you can do to improve the situation or feel better? (For example, you and your friend had a bad argument.)

→ *Again, you can't change the fact that it happened, but if there's something that could help now (such as an apology) work out what it is, decide when you can do it, and then give it no more thinking time.*

…things that might happen in the next few days or weeks? (For example, you might get picked for a school team or a boy/girl you like might ask you out.)

→ *How important is it? How much is it in your control? Is there anything you can do about it? If not, stop thinking about it. If there is, work out what action you can reasonably take and then stop thinking about it. Only think about it when it's time to act.*

...very bad things that might happen one day? (For example, someone you love being seriously ill or dying.)

It's fine to spend a few moments thinking how you'd cope if something awful happened, but then you need to try to push it away. It's very natural to worry when a disaster is reported on the news, too, and it's a good idea to talk to an adult about your fears. Try not to let it take over your thoughts. Dwelling on possible but very unlikely disasters is not useful and can make you suffer more than necessary.

...negative thoughts about yourself? (For example, anything negative about your personality, appearance, life, friendships or abilities.)

Don't spend time fretting about these things. Read the POSITIVELY YOU section again. You're changing all the time and seeing yourself through negative eyes. If it falls into the category of 'things I can't control', push it away. If you think you can control it, ask yourself whether you should have to. And if you shouldn't, push it away.

...good things that might happen? (For example, you might win lots of money or a massive competition.)

It's fun to daydream about things like that. Go for it! Some people might argue that it's a waste of time but it's good to have positive thoughts and optimism. Don't let it stop you actually doing the work that successful lives usually need, though. There's interesting research suggesting that positive daydreaming can be really useful and good for our concentration. I'll talk about that in **Just think** *on page 196.*

There is one particular time when you should definitely push bad thoughts and worries away: when you're trying to sleep. If you're losing sleep over negative thoughts, take a look at the advice about sleep on page 110, where you'll find specific suggestions for dealing with intrusive worries.

POSITIVE BOOST

Do you procrastinate? The syllable 'cras' in 'procrastination' is Latin for 'tomorrow' and 'putting things off until tomorrow' is a common habit. Is there something you know you should do? It could be as small as taking mugs downstairs from your bedroom or writing a thank you note for a birthday present. The answer is really simple: just do it. NOW! You'll feel so much better when you've got it off your mind.

★ You and control

In your notebook, draw a vertical line down the middle of the page. Write this heading on the left: **A lot of control**, and this heading on the right: **Little or no control**. Then look at the seven things on the list below and think about how much control you usually feel you have over each of them. Write each in the appropriate column, according to your personal feelings. Don't turn the page until you've done it.

★ Food and drink

★ Genes and early childhood

★ Exercise

★ Sleep

★ Mood and feelings

★ Things that happen to me

★ Stress

Now turn the page.

POSITIVELY YOU

A POSITIVE ATTITUDE

POSITIVELY HEALTHY

POSITIVELY BRAINY

POSITIVE ABOUT PEOPLE

A POSITIVE MOOD

Did your answers look like this?

★ A lot of control	★ Little or no control
Food and drink	Genes and early childhood
Exercise	Sleep
	Stress
	Things that happen to me
	Mood and feelings

That would be a common response from teenagers who don't feel they have much control over their lives. Apart from 'genes and early childhood', which obviously you can't control at all, there's no absolute right or wrong answer here and we could discuss why you *might* put the others in either column. But this book is all about helping you reach this answer:

★ A lot of control	★ Little or no control
Food and drink	Genes and early childhood
Exercise	Things that happen to me
Sleep	
Stress	
Mood and feelings	

Sleep, stress, mood and feelings are all things you can have a lot of control over.

Focus on the present: mindfulness

Let's look at tricks to help you focus your thoughts in healthy, positive ways on what you can control. Mindfulness is one good way to manage negative thoughts. It's also calming and can be great for reducing stress in busy, noisy lives.

Some schools have introduced mindfulness classes and many people of all ages find it very helpful. But people should not think it is the answer to all of today's problems. It doesn't work for everyone, so if it doesn't work for you, there's nothing wrong with you! Also, for a few people it **can** make mental conditions worse so classes should be conducted by people with appropriate training. But if you're just trying to press pause on your busy mind, then it's a good thing to practise.

What is it?

Mindfulness is a type of meditation. It encourages a focus on the present, on thoughts and feelings and senses. You can't do mindfulness while rushing around or while people are talking to you. And you can't do it while you're on social media, either! You have to devote your whole mindspace to whatever it is that you are doing and feeling at that moment.

During mindfulness practice, when a negative thought comes into your mind, you don't have to push it away. You just let it in and let it pass through your mind without trying to stop it or criticising yourself for having it. This is helpful for some people because they find it hard to push the negative thought away.

How can you bring mindfulness into your life?

Although mindfulness does need an expert teacher if you're to learn it properly, you can still practise mindful thinking and actions without special lessons. Here are two examples:

✳ Take something you're eating or drinking. Focus on it closely; notice the textures, the smells, the colours, the tastes. Notice what it feels like in your mouth, how it slips down your throat, the different taste it leaves behind. Extract every possible thought and description you can from it. Give that piece of food your entire attention for a minute.

✳ Just sit or lie in a comfortable place and listen. Listen to the sounds in your room, then draw your attention to sounds further away. Can you hear traffic? The wind? Distant voices? Electricity humming in the air? A clock ticking? A fly? Just think about them all, maybe describing them in your head? Buzzing? Humming? Clicking? Swishing?

By focusing on these simple sensations or experiences, you can calm your thoughts and push away the sense of not being in control. You have learnt to control your mind and your body, given it a break from your noisy head. You've learnt that you can – at least some of the time, when you choose – control your thoughts.

Resources

MINDFULNESS

Mindfulness for teens has some excellent resources and free apps: *mindfulnessforteens.com/resources/resources-for-mindfulness/*

AnxietyBC explains mindfulness and offers ideas: *youth.anxietybc. com/mindfulness-exercises*

Into the future
– lucky or not lucky?

We can control parts of the future but not others. We can control whether the next words we speak are kind, for example. We can control whether to put up a hand to answer a question when we know the answer (though it's harder for some people than others). But we can't control whether it rains next Saturday or whether we're going to find some money on the street next week.

Or can you? Well, there's evidence it's sometimes possible. This is all about optimism versus pessimism. An optimist expects good things to happen but a pessimist expects the worst. Of course, sometimes one of them is right and sometimes the other is right, but is it possible that how we think about the future can in some ways affect the future?

The psychologist, Richard Wiseman, in his book, *The Luck Factor*, talks about his research into the different behaviours of people who describe themselves as particularly lucky or unlucky. For one experiment, he picked Martin, who described himself as lucky, and Brenda, who thought of herself as unlucky, and set up a situation where they were asked to come separately to a café for a meeting.

The research team set this up cleverly. First, just outside the door, they put a £5 note on the pavement. Second, they arranged the tables with an actor at each, pretending to be a customer. One of these actors played the part of a successful businessman. When Martin arrived, he saw the money and picked it up, sat next to the businessman and got into conversation with him. When Brenda arrived, she didn't notice the money and, although she sat next to the same 'businessman', she didn't start a conversation. Later, when asked about their day, Martin described in great detail the interesting conversation and finding the money; Brenda didn't really have much to say about the day.

Now, this was just two people and there are many reasons why they might have behaved differently, but the point is that they had the same chances but approached them and engaged with them differently. Wiseman's book has many such stories.

You're more likely to be 'lucky' and find money if you keep your eyes open and you're more likely to make useful connections if you connect with people, aren't you?

So, maybe there are things we can do to control our 'luck' a bit: being curious and observant, being keen to join in and have a go, saying yes to opportunities, being positive. These things could help. There's the phrase 'You need to be

in it to win it'. In other words, if you don't try, you can't win.

But don't blame yourself when bad things do happen! You didn't 'fail' just because you had some bad luck. Also, don't set your goals too high, expecting everything good to happen all the time, otherwise you might often be disappointed.

Instead, try to grow a sense of, 'I'm going to approach this (day or term or competition or exam or whatever) positively. I'm going to keep alert to opportunities because then there's a really good chance of things going my way. But if they don't, never mind, next time could be better.'

Resources

LUCK AND OPTIMISM

The Luck Factor by Richard Wiseman: research involving people who consider themselves lucky or unlucky. I recommend *The Luck Factor*. It's very readable and has strategies and tips. Although aimed at adults, it's very accessible for younger people.

Here is the story of one of his experiments: *http://news.bbc.co.uk/1/hi/magazine/3335275.stm*

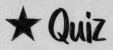 # ★ Quiz

Write your answers in your notebook or on a piece of paper or laptop:

★ How quickly can you think of three good things that have happened to you in the last year? (Big things or small things – whatever comes into your mind.)

★ How quickly can you think of three bad things that have happened to you in the last year? (Again, big or small.)

★ Which of the above questions was easier? (This gives an indication as to whether you are more optimistic or pessimistic. Of course, if some unusual bad/good things have very recently happened to you, this might affect your response.)

★ How likely do you think it is that something good will happen to you tomorrow or next week? Very/quite/don't know/quite unlikely/ very unlikely.

★ Write down three good things that might happen tomorrow or next week.

★ Write down three things you would like to achieve in the near future. (It could be this week or this term.)

★ Think about the three things you would like to achieve in the near future. What do you think are your chances of succeeding? (If you think your chances are 90–100 per cent on all of them, change two of them for more challenging ones! It would be good to have a mixture of difficulty: one where you might easily fail, one where you have a very good chance of succeeding and the other somewhere in the middle.)

For each one of your aims for the near future, write down:

★ How much will success be down to luck and how much will it be down to you?

★ Any things you will need to do if you are to have the best chance of succeeding.

★ What you will feel like if you succeed.

Now look at your answers and think about one final question:

★ Do you feel as though you have quite a lot of control over whether good things will happen to you in the next month?

Set the right goals

That point about optimism leads straight into this: we need to set goals that are just right, so we can approach the future positively and so we can succeed often enough.

If we always set goals that are too difficult, we will probably fail too often. We might even start to expect failure and too much failure risks lowering self-esteem and well-being. There's something psychologists call 'learned helplessness'. This means that if someone continually experiences being 'helpless' – either because they keep failing or because other people always do things for them and they never get the chance to succeed by themselves – they stop trying. It's like a cycle of weakness. If you have the chance to succeed by yourself, you learn what you can do, more than what you can't. And then you can set the bar a little higher each time.

If we set goals that are always too easy, we won't feel really satisfied and proud of ourselves. Also, it's important to fail *sometimes*, because it helps us become resilient. Resilience is about learning to deal with difficulty and grow stronger. I'll talk about it in more detail on page 63.

SMART goal-setting

SMART stands for these things (though in some explanations the wording differs slightly):

Specific – goals shouldn't be vague. They should be things like: 'Finish my homework by 9 pm' rather than 'Work harder'.

Measurable – you need to know when you've achieved your goal: 'Finish my homework by 9 pm' is measurable, whereas 'Work harder' isn't.

Achievable – don't set goals you can't achieve.

Relevant – there needs to be a point to what you want to do, even if only you know the point! For example, your goal might be to spot 20 different makes of car by tomorrow. If that's relevant to you and your love of cars, go for it!

Time-limited – you need an endpoint for your goal. 'I will work harder' isn't time-limited but 'I will work hard for an hour' is.

If you think about all those New Year's resolutions that people break, you'll see they're often goals such as 'I will lose weight', 'I will drink more water', 'I will stop procrastinating', 'I will exercise more'. And those break the SMART rules, so they are hard to keep.

So, think about the goals you set yourself, whether they are small ones such as, 'I will focus really well for one hour and not look at my phone' or bigger ones such as, 'I will practise the violin four times a week so that by the end of this term, I will be good enough to move to the next grade'. Set targets which will make you proud if you achieve them. And do change your goals if necessary: if you discover you've been expecting too much of yourself, go easy; if you think you can do better, raise the bar a little.

POSITIVELY YOU

A POSITIVE ATTITUDE

POSITIVELY HEALTHY

POSITIVELY BRAINY

POSITIVE ABOUT PEOPLE

A POSITIVE MOOD

POSITIVE BOOST

Write your goal down. Unless it's private, write it in big letters on a card to put above your bed or desk. Decorate it. The more effort you put into it, the more important it will feel to you. Make sure it is something you can measure and that has an end to it. If you achieve your goal, cover it with exclamation marks and stars!

Resources

GOAL SETTING

Kids Health has good general advice about goal-setting:
http://kidshealth.org/en/teens/goals-tips.html

The Teen Compass has excellent practical advice and downloadable goal-setting sheets:
www.theteencompass.org/explore/smart-goals-defined

Build resilience

Resilience is the ability to bounce back after a negative event. That could be something like failing a test or it could be a sad or scary incident. It could be small or big. Setbacks will happen to us at various points in our lives. Setbacks are unpleasant at the time, but they are useful because they allow us to grow resilience and value the good times in our lives.

People used to think resilience was like a personality trait: something you either have a lot of or a little of, something you are born with and can't control much. But psychologists now say resilience doesn't work like that: it's something we can grow.

It's certainly a good thing to have – a way of thinking that allows us to say: 'OK, so that happened. I didn't like it but I can survive it and I'll be OK in the end. In fact, I'll be stronger in the end.' It allows us not to beat ourselves up about mistakes we've made or things people have said to us and not keep dwelling on situations that were bad at the time but which are in the past.

How can you grow better resilience?

It's useful to repeat certain positive thoughts, building strong pathways in your brain. Here are some examples, which you can use whenever a relevant situation happens:

★ How I feel now is not how I will feel later – this will pass.

★ It's normal to feel sad/angry/scared now but this will pass.

★ There is someone out there to help me if I need it and it is not a sign of weakness to ask for help.

★ This will make me stronger.

★ I will be proud of my progress. Even if I take some steps backwards I will be proud of my steps forward.

★ I can take small steps, but I will get there in the end.

★ The past is the past; I can control lots of parts of the future.

★ Many people have dealt with things like this – or worse.

★ I have friends who will be happy to help me with this.

★ There will be many good moments ahead in my life.

This whole book aims to help you be more resilient by giving you practical tools to develop positively and to take things in your stride. Just believing that you can increase your control over your reactions to life's setbacks, will help build resilience.

Resources

RESILIENCE

Two useful webpages with resilience advice:

Child and Youth Health: *www.cyh.com/HealthTopics/HealthTopicDetails.aspx?p=243&np=293&id=2198*

American Psychological Association: *www.apa.org/helpcenter/bounce.aspx*

64

Build a 'growth mindset'

According to psychologist Carol Dweck, there are ways of thinking which affect our attitude towards failure and success and how pessimistic or optimistic we are and those things can affect our success. They are called 'fixed mindset' and 'growth mindset'. (A mindset is a way of thinking, attitude or set of beliefs.) Let's see which one you have and then I'll explain. Read these two paragraphs and see which one you agree with more strongly.

1. 'I believe we are born with certain skills and talents. The things I'm good or bad at now are mainly because of what I've inherited from my parents or just how my brain and body are. By now, my skills are mostly fixed and I'll always find certain subjects easier than others. So, the most sensible strategy is just to go with that and not waste time expecting to get better at things I'm rubbish at. It's too late to change! After all, Mozart was a child genius and composed his first symphony aged six and his father was a talented musician, too, so it's obvious we inherit these skills or are just lucky to be born with them. Skills and talents are mostly things we're born with; practice and teaching just develop them further.'

2. 'I believe skills and talents are things we develop and have very little to do with genes inherited from our parents. If someone is better than me at sport or music or maths or reading, it's because they've spent more time than I have on those things at an early age. Maybe their parents made them practise so they became expert at it. So that means that I can become better at anything I want to, if I spend more time practising whatever it is. After all, Mozart was so brilliant because he was trained by his father from a very early age and spent huge amounts of time practising. He threw himself into his music and that's why he was so successful at such an early age. Skills and talents mostly grow through practice and teaching.'

★ If you identify mostly with the first one, that suggests you have a fixed mindset. You believe that what you're good at is mostly luck because it's about what you're born with and other things you can't control. So, you believe that you can't *become* good at something if you haven't got the right natural talents in the first place.

★ If you identify mostly with the second, you have a growth mindset. You believe that if someone is better at something than someone else, it's mostly because of the amount of time they've spent on it, with practice and good teaching, often at an early age.

You probably sometimes have one mindset and sometimes the other, by the way. You might generally believe that you can get better with practice but sometimes find yourself thinking, 'I'll never be able to do this – I'm just not made that way'. It's quite normal to experience both types of thinking.

We have to be a bit realistic, too. You've already spent many years acquiring certain skills more than others. So, you might have really strong football or piano-playing or maths or artistic skills because you've already spent time practising. And you might have spent  less time on other things, or perhaps not been encouraged in them so much, so those skills don't feel strong.

The point is that we need to stop thinking 'I'm rubbish at this' or 'She's better than me at that' and we have to think instead, 'I can be better at this if I persevere' or 'She's only better than me because she's spent more time on it – I can change that by practising'.

It turns out that there are some things we've been forgetting or ignoring about Wolfgang Amadeus Mozart. His father was a professional music teacher and composer. Wolfgang's older sister had music lessons and when he was a very young child he seemed to love music and be interested. (Lots of toddlers are like that, especially with parents encouraging them!) So, from the age of about three, Wolfgang sat in his sister's lessons and began lessons himself as soon as possible. Again, with a keen father, this would happen easily. Also, his parents lost five children, so a huge amount of attention would have been showered on Wolfgang and his sister. From the earliest age, he lived and breathed music, learning with the best teachers and performing regularly.

We are told that he started composing at the age of five, but what does that mean? His father's handwriting is on his early works, so it's not clear what he did himself. His father made money from his children's performances so we might guess that there may have been exaggeration as he billed them both as 'child prodigies'. Mozart was certainly an exceptionally brilliant musician – quite possibly the best the world has seen – but everything in his life points towards the best environment for that to happen: good teaching, plenty of encouragement and lots and lots of practice. There is no proof that he was 'born like that'.

Now that we know so much more about how learning and expertise happen, it's more likely that, even if there were such a thing as a 'natural talent' or the 'genes for genius', without vast hours of practice and good teaching, this natural talent wouldn't appear.

So, think yourself into a growth mindset by focusing on the idea that perseverance and hard work are far better ways to predict success. And you'll feel much prouder if you've achieved it yourself rather than having it given to you by a fairy when you were a baby!

Resources

<u>FIXED AND GROWTH MINDSETS</u>

Carol Dweck's work:
http://big-change.org/growth-mindset-research-2/ and https://www.mindsetworks.com/science/

Matthew Syed, author of *Bounce*:
www.matthewsyed.co.uk/2015/09/16/the-power-of-learning-from-your-mistakes/

Syed's TED talk encouraging people to acknowledge failure and confront mistakes: *https://www.youtube.com/watch?v=MmVCYqs3mko*

Malcolm Gladwell's book, *Outliers*, popularised the idea that 10,000 hours of practice are needed to be expert in a complex task, such as violin playing. This article explains his view: *http://wisdomgroup.com/blog/10000-hours-of-practice/*

Gladwell based his idea on research by Professor Anders Ericsson but Ericsson has distanced himself from Gladwell's conclusions, as this article explains. Ten thousand hours was offered by Ericsson as an average, varying greatly between people and between tasks. Many other factors are important, such as determination, good teaching and also the type of practice. Ericsson says it's not the quantity of practice but the quality that matters most: *www.makeuseof.com/tag/10000-hour-rule-wrong-really-master-skill/*

POSITIVELY YOU

A POSITIVE ATTITUDE

POSITIVELY HEALTHY

POSITIVELY BRAINY

POSITIVE ABOUT PEOPLE

A POSITIVE MOOD

Notice what went well

This is a brilliant strategy for a positive attitude from the world of positive psychology and is based on strong research. (You'll find references to it in the **Resources** on page 72.) It deals with the problem that we spend too much time thinking about what went wrong. If we do this too much, we spiral into negativity and anxiety and miss opportunities to be optimistic and in control.

One thing, though: it's also perfectly healthy to think about 'what went wrong'. That's how we can try to make sure it doesn't happen again, if there's something we can do differently. So, I'm not saying you shouldn't think about those things, too. Just make sure you spend *more* time thinking about what went *right*.

Here's how to do it. Set aside a few minutes before you go to bed each night and do the simple things in the box below. Lots of research, notably by Martin Seligman and colleagues, shows that this simple daily act can have a hugely positive effect on many aspects of well-being and health. And it's a brilliant way to relax before sleep.

★ What went well?

Identify three good things that happened today. They can be big things, such as doing well in a test or winning a team game. Or they can be really small, such as having your favourite food at lunch or sitting in the playground with the sun on your back.

Then say why each one happened. It could be that you did well in a test because you worked hard. It could be that you had your favourite food at lunch because you were lucky that day.

Finally, say which of your character strengths you used. (See **Know and value your 'character strengths'** on page 30.) Did you use Perseverance or Bravery? Hope or Gratitude? Love of Learning or Creativity? You probably used a combination. Acknowledge them!

But what if you have something really difficult happening in your life?

I'm afraid bad things happen to good people as well as bad people and there's no doubt that some events can be really hard to deal with. Whatever life has thrown at you and your family, you can't change the past. So, try to leave it where it is: behind you. And focus on some things you *can* do. Here are some tips:

✳ If it's a new situation, realise that time is a great healer – it's a cliché but it is true! That's not saying you'll 'get over it', just that your feelings will change and the pain will fade.

✳ If it's a long-term situation, you will be able to find a 'new normal' even if it takes time.

✳ If it's something you can't control, spend as little time as possible thinking about it, and especially not the time when you're trying to go to sleep.

✳ Build lots of positive things into your life, small activities that give you a break from the bad stuff. Like sunshine in winter.

POSITIVELY YOU

A POSITIVE ATTITUDE

POSITIVELY HEALTHY

POSITIVELY BRAINY

POSITIVE ABOUT PEOPLE

A POSITIVE MOOD

✱ Even with difficult stuff going on, you're allowed to laugh! Laughter is very good medicine. It releases endorphins – chemicals in the brain that are often called 'happy chemicals' – and you feel more upbeat.

✱ If you find your situation really hard, talk to a trusted adult. A teacher is a very good start because they are trained in how to respond. They might not have the answers themselves but they know how to help you find them. Counsellors are specially trained to help you process your thoughts in a healthy way.

✱ Use this book to understand how to have control and develop a growth mindset: huge tasks can be managed if we take one step at a time – every long journey begins with one step; our talents are not gifts we're born with but things we develop through practice. So, be determined and you can beat anything life throws at you. And then you will feel proud – and rightly so!

Resources

WHAT WENT WELL

Research about the effectiveness of focusing on what went well comes from psychologists led by Martin Seligman. His 'Three Blessings' exercise is here, along with an exercise called a 'Gratitude Visit': *www.brainpickings.org/2014/02/18/martin-seligman-gratitude-visit-three-blessings/*

He also talks about this on Action for Happiness, which has excellent resources: *http://www.actionforhappiness.org/take-action/find-three-good-things-each-day*

An article by Seligman for the BBC where he explains the science behind this: *news.bbc.co.uk/1/hi/programmes/happiness_formula/4903464.stm*

Summing up

Attitude is one of those things you might have thought you couldn't control. In this section you've learnt a load of things you positively can!

We began with ways you can control negative thoughts, thinking about which ones are useful, and which are not, and seeing whether you might calm anxiety and your busy brain with mindfulness techniques.

You've thought about how perhaps an optimistic attitude can affect your luck. You've learnt how to set sensible goals which will help you towards success and how to value the things that have gone well for you.

Importantly, by understanding that it's grit and determination more than talent and luck that brings success, you've given yourself a growth mindset instead of a fixed one.

These are big ideas but they're also simple and well-researched. They will help you approach your teenage years with excitement, curiosity and positivity.

Positively Healthy

If we want to have good mental and physical well-being, an important part of that is looking after our bodies. The choices we make about food, drink, exercise, fresh air and sleep all make big differences to how well we feel and how our bodies works for us.

When you were a young child, your parents or carers made all these decisions for you and you didn't have very much choice, but now you can start to take control of these things.

There are so many ways of giving yourself the best chance of staying healthy and that's what this section is all about. I hope you'll find it really empowering, too, as you learn the facts you need to make the best choices. It's your body and your life!

Eat well

The great news is that you don't have to eat things you don't like! Eating well doesn't involve dieting and it's not boring, pointless, expensive or difficult. It takes a bit of knowledge (coming up) and a bit of thinking (you can do that) and then you'll be set up with habits to help you be as healthy as possible, for life.

Another good thing is that it's an area of your life where you can very easily take control. And whoever does all the food shopping and preparing in your house will probably welcome you getting involved in the choices. Making good choices about food is one way you can approach your teenage years positively and strongly.

We don't have to make perfect choices every time and there's nothing wrong with eating something junky every now and then. It's about information and balance. It's about knowing how to fill your body with enough fantastic, tasty food so that you get all the nutrients you need. If you do that, you'll benefit your brain, mental health, physical health, learning, mood, skin, eyes, teeth, digestion and energy levels. Just with food!

What happens if you make right or wrong choices?

There are long-term effects and more immediate ones. It's hard to be very enthusiastic about long-term ones because they are so vague and distant: 'having less risk of cancer and other illnesses', 'having stronger bones', 'being healthier' may be excellent aims but it's difficult to stay motivated when you can't see quick results.

Let's focus on one that you can notice immediately: how you feel. Good food choices make a noticeable difference to how you feel for the rest of the day. They affect energy and concentration, mood and emotional and physical feelings. If you eat a sugary snack, for example, it gives you a burst of energy but within minutes that energy is spent and you're hungry again, and maybe dizzy and snappy. Your concentration suffers and so does your mood. But make a different choice – yogurt with oats or a banana on top; a tuna, egg or chicken sandwich; a bowl of porridge; a handful of nuts – and you'll have energy and concentration for far longer. This section is all about these choices.

So, what are the super-brain foods?

There is no one magic food that makes brains and bodies work brilliantly. We need a vast number of nutrients – the 'useful' parts of foods that nourish us – and no particular food contains all of them. It's true that some contain more nutrients than others, and I'll come to those in a minute, but I just want to say now: don't pay too much attention to headlines saying that Brazil nuts/blueberries/porridge are 'The Answer' to a brilliant brain. They are part of the answer, as you'll see, but only a part. (And don't worry if you don't like Brazil nuts, blueberries or porridge, because there are other options!)

Another reason for not bothering too much about anything claimed as a 'super-food for the brain' is that there's the temptation to consume lots of it and that's a bad idea: if you eat huge quantities of one thing, you won't be able to eat enough of other things. It's all about balance. Also, just because something is good for us, or necessary, doesn't mean that *masses* of it is even better than a 'normal' amount. Overeating even the healthiest foods can cause problems.

There are three main things to think about:

1. Eating enough
2. Having plenty of variety
3. Making enough positive choices.

1. EATING ENOUGH

We need to eat enough because our bodies and brains can't work when we don't. Food gives us energy and our bodies and brains use – 'burn' – that energy for everything we do: not just physical things like running and swimming; but mental things like reading, writing, working out problems; and automatic things like breathing, regulating temperature and reacting to stress. We also need energy for growing and repairing cells, and we use it while sleeping, too. Even if we lie in bed all day, we use energy; but actively using our bodies and brains means we use more.

That energy comes from calories – nowhere else. So, you need enough calories. If you don't, obviously you'll lose weight but you may also slow the natural processes which keep your body healthy. So, if you need to lose weight you should do this slowly and under medical supervision to make sure you're not harming yourself.

POSITIVELY YOU

A POSITIVE ATTITUDE

POSITIVELY HEALTHY

POSITIVELY BRAINY

POSITIVE ABOUT PEOPLE

A POSITIVE MOOD

How many calories should you consume?

Don't count calories! Let me explain.

First, the only people who should count calories are those who've been put on a 'calorie-controlled' diet by a qualified medical expert. In that case, you'll be told how many calories you need. How much a person needs depends on: height; other aspects of size such as bone size or frame; gender; age; level of exercise. So I can't say how many calories you need because I don't know those things about you. Not having enough calories can cause you harm.

Second, counting calories can lead to an obsessive attitude to food and that isn't healthy. I don't want you to control food intake like that: it's painful, negative and unhelpful because not all calories behave in the same way. Calories from some foods are processed and turned into energy quickly while calories from other foods take longer to be processed. So, looking at the calorie content of something is not enough to tell you whether you're making a healthy choice.

How do you know if you're eating enough?

If you're a healthy weight, you're probably eating enough. You can find out whether you are a healthy weight by looking at an online chart for your height and age. This usually measures your 'BMI' (Body Mass Index) and there's a different ideal range for different genders and ages. Take a look at the links in the **Resources** on page 86.

What if you're hungry all the time? Does that mean you're not eating enough? Well, it might. Or it might be that you're not making the best choices, because some foods (processed sugary ones, for example) turn into energy so fast that the energy can quickly be used up and you're hungry again.

What if your weight is too high? Does that mean you're eating *too much*? Well, it might. Or it might be that, again, you're not making the best choices.

If you're worrying whether you might be eating too much or too little, ask an adult with medical training, such as a school nurse or your GP. But if you're just wondering but not worrying, I suggest you follow the advice below (**Having plenty of variety** and **Making enough positive choices**) because if you're doing those things and you're within healthy weight guidelines for your age and height, and you have enough energy for daily life, you're probably eating the right amount.

I'm emphasising eating *enough* because some people your age restrict their food in the hope of being thinner. That's not how to have a healthy body and brain and certainly not how to be positively teenage! Being healthy means eating an amount of food that keeps the body and brain working well and while you're growing you need more food to fuel that growth.

Also, sometimes young people who feel they are growing too tall think that if they eat less they won't grow so tall: but height is mostly controlled by genes and things that happened during your very early years so you can't change that now. Restricting your food now just risks you not having the nutrients for good skin, nails, eyes, hair, digestion and all the other things your body needs.

2. HAVING PLENTY OF VARIETY
Eating a rainbow

One of the best ways to have variety is to 'eat a rainbow': foods of lots of different colours. (This does *not* mean Smarties or M&Ms or other food that's artificially coloured!) Think of all the different colours in these foods: strawberries, bananas, purple grapes, carrots, tomatoes, sweetcorn, peas, oranges, cucumber, yogurt. The colours are produced by the different nutrients they each have so it's simple to choose a variety of colours without needing to know what's in them. And if you don't like the suggestions in that list, there are so many other things you can choose. Just look for foods that are coloured by nature.

POSITIVELY YOU

A POSITIVE ATTITUDE

POSITIVELY HEALTHY

POSITIVELY BRAINY

POSITIVE ABOUT PEOPLE

A POSITIVE MOOD

All the food groups

Another way to get variety is to make sure you select from different food groups. You needn't have every group at every meal – though it's good to aim for it – but over a day you'd want a good balance of them all. There are five main groups and further down you'll see lots of examples of where to find each one:

✳ Fruit and veg: containing many vitamins as well as fibre to fill us up and help digestion.

✳ Other carbohydrates: important for quick energy. (Fruit and veg are mostly carbs, too, but this group consists of things like rice, pasta and bread.)

✳ Protein: important for growing and rebuilding cells but also a great carrier of energy and longer-lasting than many carbs; keeps hunger away for longer.

✳ Dairy: usually from cows but all animal milk products are dairy. It contains protein and important vitamins and minerals such as calcium, essential for strong bones. Your calcium intake as a teenager is important later in life. If you have a health reason for restricting dairy, you still need these nutrients, so get expert advice about alternatives.

✳ Fats: as a rule, the important fats are found in plants and oily fish. They are an essential part of our diet, partly because they help us absorb other nutrients.

If there's any food you can't eat for medical reasons, don't worry: there are always other ways to get the goodness you need. Or if you're vegetarian, vegan or anyone else who avoids certain foods, get advice about how to eat well. You'll find **Resources** about food on page 86.

3. MAKING ENOUGH POSITIVE CHOICES

It's best not to think about 'good foods' and 'bad foods' because then you can start feeling guilty, which is unnecessary. Think about 'foods I should have plenty of' and 'foods I should only have occasionally'. The main trick is to find enough foods that you *like* in that first category. Then you'll fill yourself up on those.

Foods to have plenty of:

Fruit and veg

* Any fruit and veg! Especially veg, as it's less sweet

* Some vegetables to try: broccoli, spinach, lettuce, carrots, beetroot, peas, corn, beans of any sort, sweet potato

* Some fruits to consider especially: berries (blueberries and blackcurrants are fantastic), tomatoes, apples, bananas – all these contain good quantities of a variety of essential nutrients.

Protein-rich foods

* Fish – any fish but especially tuna, mackerel, salmon and herring

* Chicken – go easy on deep-fried chicken and avoid chicken (or other meat) that has been 'processed' in a factory into pies, sausages, and sliced meat that has been 'reformed'. But roast chicken, stir-fry or baked chicken breasts or thighs are all good

* Beans, lentils, tofu, soya – these are really important parts of our diet but especially for vegetarians and vegans

* Nuts and seeds

* Eggs – the yolk contains iron and the white is high in protein and low in fat.

POSITIVELY YOU

A POSITIVE ATTITUDE

POSITIVELY HEALTHY

POSITIVELY BRAINY

POSITIVE ABOUT PEOPLE

A POSITIVE MOOD

✳ Carbohydrates and wholegrains (grains also contain a good source of protein but you'd need a lot to get enough protein just from grains)

✳ Rice – choose non-white if you can; or mix brown and white

✳ Pasta – again, brown pasta is better

✳ Potatoes – especially with skins on

✳ Oats – porridge is a great way to start the day

✳ Wholegrain cereals – avoid processed sweetened cereals.

Dairy

✳ Milk

✳ Yogurt – avoid highly sweetened ones; avoid low-fat or reduced-fat varieties, as they usually contain extra sugar or sweetener

✳ Cheese.

Fats

✳ Oils – olive, sunflower, flaxseed, grapeseed, canola and nut; they lose nutrients when cooked so having them as a salad dressing is even better

✳ Oily fish – tuna, mackerel, salmon, herring

✳ Avocadoes

✳ Nuts.

Food to have occasionally:

These foods won't do harm in small quantities, but try not to have them every day. Because it's important to be positive about foods rather than guilty, I'm going to keep this simple and painless by giving you only a very small list:

✳ Fizzy or sugary drinks

✳ Sweets and chocolate

✳ Crisps

✳ Highly processed foods such as sausages and pies.

My philosophy is that if you eat enough of the positive choices, you'll be full up and you won't crave sweet or processed things. And there's nothing wrong with a cake or ice-cream if you've had a good portion of nutritious stuff first.

See page 85 for a stack of ideas about how you can actually incorporate those great choices into your day.

Are you a very fussy eater?

It's OK! It's very common to be cautious about new tastes and to have lots of things you really don't like. Can you find eight things in the list of foods on pages 81–2 that you like or at least don't dislike? If you can, there's no problem – just eat lots of them! Eat them first, so that you can eat as much of them as possible, then do your best to gradually grow your range of tastes. Set yourself a challenge of liking one more thing by next month. Don't let food become a battleground. There are hundreds and hundreds of possibilities and many more than I've suggested.

Do you need supplements?

If you eat a good range of the foods I've suggested, you will get everything you need from your diet. Food supplements are not cheap and could be a waste of money. But some people may need them. If you fall into any of the categories below, get expert advice to make sure you're healthy and ask whether you need supplements:

Vegans or other dietary choices which restrict a wide range of foods: it's not difficult to get all your nutrients from a vegan or almost any diet but you need to find sources of calcium, Vitamin B12 and iron. Get advice from relevant national societies for vegetarians, vegans, etc.

✱ Girls who have started their periods: if you have heavy blood loss you can lack iron. (See your doctor and don't take iron supplements without medical advice, as too much is not good for you. Iron is found in egg yolks and dark green vegetables, as well as some red meat, but red meat is something we're told not to eat too often.)

✱ People who can't do much weight-bearing exercise: you may need extra calcium and Vitamin D to help build bone mass. (Weight-bearing exercise means exercise that you do while supporting your own body weight on your legs or arms. People who have joint problems, weight problems or disabilities which require a wheelchair fall into this category.)

✱ People who don't get much natural sunlight on their body (if they live in a very cold climate or don't go outside much) or people with dark skins (because melanin in their skin can block sunlight): sunlight helps the body produce Vitamin D so these people may need supplements.

✱ People with a specific medical condition that stops them producing or processing certain nutrients: you will know if this applies to you.

SNACK IDEAS	SNACK IDEAS	MEAL IDEAS	MEAL IDEAS
dried berries	yogurt	lentil/veg soup + cheese roll	eggs + whole grain toast
mixed seeds/ nuts	tuna paté or hummus + oatcakes	fish pie + salad	egg/tuna sandwich + salad
Brazil nuts	cheese + tomato sandwich	whole grain salad roll + rice pudding	cheese/egg/ chicken salad
home-made flapjack	avocado dip + carrots	porridge + boiled egg	chicken/tuna + pasta + salad
banana/ carrot cake	peanut butter on bagel	lentil bake + yogurt	baked beans on toast
banana	apple + rice cake + cheese	baked aubergine + cheese on top	quiche + salad
shake with banana/ berries	Marmite sandwich	wholewheat pancakes with fruit or savoury stuffing	baked potato + cheese/ beans + salad
dried fruit	bagel + cream cheese	salmon/ mackerel/tuna + rice + peppers	salmon/tuna + rice + peas/ salad
oatcakes + cheese	cottage cheese and breadsticks	stir-fry chicken, veg + noodles	nut roast + wholemeal roll
milk or hot chocolate	home-made granola	chicken curry + rice + fruit salad	couscous + grilled chicken + salad

POSITIVELY YOU

A POSITIVE ATTITUDE

POSITIVELY HEALTHY

POSITIVELY BRAINY

POSITIVE ABOUT PEOPLE

A POSITIVE MOOD

POSITIVE BOOST

Take a fuel-boosting snack to school. Fill a plastic box with nuts (if your school allows them), seeds, dried or fresh fruit, Marmite sticks, home-made flapjack, or oatcakes with cheese, though you'll need to eat this during the morning. If you can't manage breakfast before leaving home, you can eat this snack when you get to school.

And if you're hungry now, EAT!

Resources

EATING WELL

Healthy weight and BMI

Teens Health, part of the Kids Health website, has two places to calculate your BMI and find healthy advice:

http://kidshealth.org/en/teens/bmi.html

https://nccd.cdc.gov/dnpabmi/calculator.aspx

Healthy eating for teenagers

From the NHS: http://www.nhs.uk/Livewell/Goodfood/Pages/ healthy-eating-teens.aspx

From Kids Health: *http://kidshealth.org/en/teens/food-fitness/*

This one is from the US and has a Spanish version: *https://www. healthychildren.org/English/ages-stages/teen/nutrition/Pages/A-Teenagers-Nutritional-Needs.aspx*

Vegetarian and vegan health

From the NHS: *http://www.nhs.uk/Livewell/Vegetarianhealth/Pages/ Vegandiets.aspx*

From the Vegetarian Resource Group: *http://www.vrg.org/nutrition/ teennutrition.htm*

Keep hydrated

You've often been told to drink plenty of water, to prevent you becoming 'dehydrated' – literally 'lacking water'. It's fairly easy if you like drinking plain water because that's certainly good for you. But you still need to think about how *much* water you need.

Also, what about other drinks? All liquids are basically water but some liquids are less good at keeping us 'hydrated' than others.

You'll find the facts about keeping hydrated and helpful suggestions about what to drink, right here. So, read on!

How much water?

It depends how quickly you're losing water (through sweating, breathing and peeing) and that depends on how hot you are or how active. You get thirstier when it's hotter or when you're doing exercise. Feeling thirsty is the obvious sign that you need to drink more.

The other thing that makes it complicated is that any guidelines you read *include* water in other drinks and in food. And it can be really hard to work that out!

I'll give you two guidelines to help you decide whether you're drinking enough:

First: if you feel thirsty, you should definitely drink something. And you shouldn't wait to become very thirsty – ideally, aim to drink enough to *prevent* feeling thirsty. Keep some water with you when you can and drink more in hot weather or when you're doing physical exercise.

Second: health organisations suggest we aim for at least six glasses (1.2 litres) of liquid a day in cool weather and eight glasses (2 litres) in warm weather or during activity. These figures are based on UK (six glasses) and US (eight glasses) government guidelines. You'll read arguments about which is right or even whether either of them is right, but it is at least good to know what the 'official' guidelines are.

You'll hear people say it's a myth that drinking water is good for us: it's not a myth! Drinking water is essential. What is *not* certain is whether drinking eight glasses is better than drinking six (or any other number you can come up with.) Remember all the time that these figures *include* water in food and other drinks. I do think it's best not to obsess, though: just aim to drink enough so that you don't get to the thirsty stage.

What makes it more complicated is that we need to think about which drinks are 'better' than others at giving us the right amount of water. Let's look at that now.

What drinks count?

All drinks are made mostly of water – that's how they're liquid. In fact, most foods contain a lot of water. For example, an apple is about 85 per cent water. So, if you ate enough apples, in theory you'd have enough water. But getting all your water from apples would mean you'd eat more apples than was good for you! You'd probably get a sore stomach and if you did it regularly, you wouldn't have enough other nutrients.

It does matter where we get our water. The simplest way is to drink plain water. Some other drinks are fine but some have a few disadvantages, and we need to be aware of those. Then we can choose whether to drink them freely or drink less. So, let's look at the facts about various drinks.

Milk – a really healthy drink for most people; it certainly contributes well to water intake but also has other nutrients. Whether you choose full-cream, semi-skimmed or skimmed will depend on whether you are underweight or overweight, but semi-skimmed is appropriate for most people. There are alternatives to dairy milk – such as almond, coconut or soya – but these are often expensive. Experts disagree as to whether soya is good or bad, particularly in large quantities, and I suggest you talk to a dietician if you are planning to drink it or eat soya bean products.

Fruit or herbal teas and other caffeine-free teas – fine as an alternative to some of your water intake.

Fruit juice – whether from concentrate or freshly squeezed juice, fruit juices all contain acid (which is bad for teeth) and sugar. Even pure fruit juice with no added sugar still contains the natural sugar of the fruit. Also, sugar requires extra water to digest. So, for many reasons, you shouldn't drink *too much* fruit juice, though a glass a day isn't a problem if you clean your teeth afterwards. Ideally, drink juice with a meal rather than on its own. Fruit juice also has vitamins and a small amount of fibre if you drink juice with 'bits' in. All this also applies to smoothies.

Diluting fruit juice or 'squash' – choose varieties that have no added sugar or artificial colours. The artificial sweeteners that replace the sugar in these drinks also risk health problems and we are advised not to consume too much. So, whether you have sugar-free or sugary varieties, don't drink too often and, when you do, dilute with as much water as possible. You can get used to drinking it very dilute and eventually you might find you just prefer water. Water with a slice of lemon, lime or orange is wonderful.

Fizzy/carbonated drinks – only for occasional treats as there are some important problems: many contain a lot of sugar; the 'diet' varieties contain large quantities of artificial sweeteners; they are not good for our teeth; and they often contain caffeine.

Caffeine – found in coffee, most teas and some fizzy drinks (such as energy drinks and cola). One problem with caffeine is that it is a 'diuretic', which means that it takes water from your body by making you pee more. This means you need to drink more liquid to replace the liquid that the caffeine removed. Experts say that if you drink a cup of any drink with caffeine in, you should only count it as half a cup of water. Caffeine raises your heart rate and wakes you up, too, so avoid it completely during the evening.

Alcohol – I know you're not drinking alcohol but I want to mention it anyway, so you know for the future. It's a diuretic, as well as having other serious health disadvantages. Alcohol doesn't count at all towards water intake. Tell your parents!

What happens if we don't drink enough water?

Every part of your body needs enough water and you're losing it all the time, when you go to the toilet, when you sweat and every time you breathe. But the first things you'd probably notice would be headaches, feeling dizzy and losing some concentration. You'll find it harder to do your best work. The brain has more water content than other parts of the body and that may be why it needs water to keep it functioning well. Take a few swigs of water and you'll feel better almost immediately! Your headache may take a little longer to go, but keeping your fluid levels up will help you focus and feel better.

Can we drink too much water?

Yes. Blood needs a complicated balance of salts, minerals and chemicals. If you drink *far* too much water, you dilute that balance and become unwell. But you really need to drink a lot before you'd have a problem, so it's not likely. Don't force yourself to drink.

If you're drinking a lot but still feeling thirsty, even when you're not exercising or feeling hot, see a doctor, just in case you have a problem, such as diabetes.

A word about salt

Salt makes us thirsty. How it does this is clever: first, salt removes water from the blood (making our blood thicker and less watery); because this isn't healthy, the body deals with this by making us feel thirsty so we drink more.

Salt can be a pretty unhealthy thing to eat (though we do need some of it) and if we eat lots of salty things we can get so used to it that we need more. But reducing our salt intake can be difficult because so many foods are high in salt: crisps and most savoury snacks, most processed food, most bread, most takeaways, and many tinned foods such as baked beans. It's often hidden in foods that don't even taste particularly salty.

Being careful about salt is even more important for adults – tell yours! People with high blood pressure should be extra careful. But for most people the best thing is not to try to eliminate it completely but not to add salt to things and to go easy on the foods that really do taste salty. Drink extra water if you do eat something salty.

POSITIVE BOOST

Most people prefer iced water to warm. Make some flavoured ice-cubes by putting a small piece of any of the following into the spaces in an ice-tray before filling with water: lemon, lime or orange slice; mint or lemon balm leaf; fruit. It's fun and simple to do and the act of making it gives you the chance to be creative and take a few moments out of your busy life.

Resources

DRINKING ENOUGH

This is a good site from Australia: www.healthykids.nsw.gov.au/kids-teens/stats-and-facts-teens/teens-nutrition/drinks-for-hydration.aspx

An important page from the UK NHS talks about whether it is a myth that you have to drink as much water as we are told: www.nhs.uk/news/2011/07July/Pages/eight-glasses-of-water-a-day.aspx

An interesting article showing that we need to keep hydrated, but don't need to count eight glasses of water to do it: www.care2.com/greenliving/8-common-myths-about-dehydration.html

The power of oxygen

O_2 Oxygen is in the air we breathe, of course. Without it, we quickly die. We don't have to think about breathing, but there are a couple of situations where you might not be getting the ideal amount of oxygen. If you are aware of this, it's very easy to deal with it. The strategies I'll give you will make an instant difference to how you feel and how your brain and body work.

It's useful to think about what is in the air we breathe. We tend to say that we breathe in oxygen and breathe out carbon dioxide. But the truth is more complicated. The air we breathe in is mostly nitrogen (about 78 per cent), while oxygen makes up about 20 per cent. There are other gases, including a small amount of carbon dioxide. The figures change depending on how high above sea level we are, and other factors. Up a mountain, the oxygen will be much less. So, the air we breathe in does not always contain the same amount of oxygen.

Assuming you're not about to climb a mountain, let's look at two situations where you might have less oxygen than ideal. (By the way, people who live up mountains adapt to less oxygen and they can manage well!)

POSITIVELY YOU

A POSITIVE ATTITUDE

POSITIVELY HEALTHY

POSITIVELY BRAINY

POSITIVE ABOUT PEOPLE

A POSITIVE MOOD

First, think about times when you've been sitting in a room for a while. Maybe it's your bedroom at home and the door and window are shut or maybe it's a classroom with lots of people breathing the same air. Since you breathe in oxygen and breathe out carbon dioxide, after a time there's not as much oxygen in the room as there was. It feels 'stuffy' and airless. There's more carbon dioxide and less oxygen.

The simple strategy is to get up, go out of the room and have a very short walk or do something a bit energetic like walking up some stairs. Obviously, you might not be able to do this in the middle of a lesson! But even asking to open the window will help. Many teachers understand about this and they find that getting students to stand up and walk around or do some running on the spot makes them able to work better afterwards.

Moving around makes your heart and breathing faster, so more oxygen goes through your lungs. From there, the oxygen is carried in your blood, all around your body, including your brain.

Basically, the first tip is: if you've been sitting down for a while, get up, move around and ideally go outside. This also applies if you've been sitting down for computer games, video games, or any use of your smartphone or other device. This can become really unhealthy for body and brain so one very important positively healthy tip is: avoid sitting down for longer than an hour at a time.

Second, when you are stressed or nervous, your breathing will probably become too shallow. Try this activity to test your breathing right now:

Keep breathing just as you were. Put one hand high on your chest, with your thumb at the base of your throat, and the other hand below your ribcage, on your stomach. Just breathe normally a few times. Which hand moves more? If it's the higher hand, your breathing is too shallow – you may be too anxious and stressed. You won't be getting enough oxygen into your

POSITIVE BOOST

If you've been sitting for a while, get up now. Stretch as tall as you can, breathing deeply and slowly. As you breathe in, raise your arms high into the air. As you breathe out, bring them slowly down while stretching them to the side in a big arc. Do this a few times. Then go for a two-minute walk around the house. Do this whenever you've been working for more than 45 minutes at home.

Or, if you can't go outside, lie on your back. Raise your knees towards your chest, roll your hips upwards so they are off the ground; place your hands beneath your hips; and do some upside down cycling with your legs.

body and you may feel a bit dizzy or your concentration may start to fail. Relaxed breathing is sometimes called 'belly breathing' because it's the 'belly' that moves more. That sort of breathing tends to be slower and deeper.

So, deep breathing will help you get more oxygen into your blood stream. Don't do it too much, too deeply or for too long though, or you might feel faint or even actually faint, as the oxygen and carbon dioxide levels in your blood become imbalanced.

Sleeping with a window open is a good idea. Of course, it isn't always possible but do try it if you can. There are special locks and fastenings that mean the window can only be opened a tiny bit for safety.

Just getting outside to inhale fresher air can make you feel much better instantly. It clears your head, helps you focus, improves mood and generally affects your physical and mental health in positive ways.

POSITIVELY YOU

A POSITIVE ATTITUDE

POSITIVELY HEALTHY

POSITIVELY BRAINY

POSITIVE ABOUT PEOPLE

A POSITIVE MOOD

Sunlight on your skin

Sunlight helps the body produce Vitamin D, essential for strong bones. That's because calcium builds strong bones but without Vit D the calcium isn't properly absorbed.

People who don't have enough Vit D can have weaker bones and might develop a condition called rickets, where bones become softer and may bend outwards – 'bowed legs'. Rickets was common amongst people with poor diets before we knew about Vit D and it's still quite common in colder countries and poorer communities. Vit D may also protect against serious illnesses later. Because of all this, it's often added to 'fortified' cereals. To see whether it's in the cereal you eat, look at the list of nutrients on the packet. That's one way to get Vit D but those cereals often also contain a lot of sugar so we shouldn't have too much of them.

We get some Vit D from food but it's hard to get enough that way because, apart from those cereals, it's only in a small number of foods (oily fish, some red meat and eggs) so we really need sunlight. Besides, it feels great to have a bit of sunlight on our skin. It usually raises people's spirits!

One problem, however, is that sunburn is dangerous, causing long-term damage to skin and extra risk of skin cancer later. So, how can you get the right amount safely?

First, spend enough time outside. (Looking through a window doesn't help because the 'UVB' rays don't go through glass.) In a cold climate, this can be difficult, especially in winter months. But try to go outside each day if you can.

Second, expose more than just your face, which is hard if you need to bundle yourself up in coat and gloves. When you can, roll your sleeves up and your socks down and get that sunlight on your skin.

Third, go outside even when it's not sunny. If you're outside on a moderately dull day, there's still some light coming through the clouds. When the sun is higher (between 11 am and 3 pm) you have more chance of getting enough sunlight.

Fourth, everyone's needs are different. If you have darker skin – Asian or African colouring, for example – you need to spend longer in the sun to make the same amount of Vit D, but even people with very dark skins can still burn, so be careful.

How to make sure you don't burn

Different skin types make a huge difference to how much sun is safe. Younger skins tend to be more delicate, too. Here are some things which mean you have to be more careful than other people in the sun, as you are at greater risk of sunburn and skin cancers later:

✳ Skin that tends to go pink in the sun easily

✳ Lots of moles or freckles

✳ Fair or light colouring – blonde hair, blue eyes and pale skin

✳ A history of skin cancer in your family.

But people with darker skins can still burn and are at risk of all the same problems; it's just that they can tolerate the sun for a little longer.

Sunburn risk isn't only when the weather is obviously hot and sunny. It depends on some other things, too:

✱ Time of year: in the UK and northern Europe, the sun is closest to you between April and September; near the equator, it's close to you all year round; in the southern parts of South America or southern Australia it would be closest between November and March

✱ Altitude – if you're up mountains, you're closer to the sun

✱ Whether the cloud is thick or thin

✱ If you are on sand, snow or water, some of the sun's rays are reflected back at you, giving you more exposure.

People very often get sunburnt when they are not sunbathing. They might be doing an activity, not feeling particularly hot, and just not thinking about the sun. Often, a breeze makes us feel nice and cool, but the sun can be doing its damage anyway.

Another useful thing is to look out for the 'UV index' for the day. You'll find this on the Internet, on weather apps and on weather reports during the summer months wherever you are in the world.

Don't take risks with the sun: use a high-factor suncream and don't expose your skin to the sun for too long. You can still burn through light cloud and a cool breeze can stop you noticing how hot it is. Go outside for short periods at a time and don't wait to feel tingling or redness before you cover up or go in.

A suntan is a sign of damage. So, what we're aiming for is to get enough sunlight but without having any visible effects. Little and often is the key.

Do you need to take Vit D supplements?

During summer months, most people won't need supplements, unless you are unable to go outdoors much or you cover your skin outside for cultural or other reasons.

During the winter, especially if you spend most of your time indoors, or if there's any reason why you don't get much sunlight, it could be a good idea.

Studies over the last ten years suggest that a significant and growing percentage of the UK population is Vit D deficient – anything between 25 per cent and 70 per cent depending on what measurements you use – particularly in the north of the country. It looks as though there's a growing problem in the US, too, and that deficiency amongst young people is increasing in various countries.

Only an expert can confirm whether this is an issue for you: discuss with a school nurse, doctor or a dietician. It will depend on your diet, skin type, where you live and your individual health. There will be no harm in taking the recommended amount as a supplement, but never take more than that unless advised by an expert. And remember that it's always best to try to get the right amount of nutrients naturally, not from supplements. Taking too much of certain vitamins can be dangerous.

Resources

HEALTHY USE OF THE SUN

How to know whether your skin type is more likely to burn and the facts you need, from Cancer Research UK: www.cancerresearchuk.org/about-cancer/causes-of-cancer/sun-uv-and-cancer/am-i-at-risk-of-sunburn

And a US site: www.senseaboutscienceusa.org/sun-risk-skin-cancer-different-groups/

POSITIVELY YOU

A POSITIVE ATTITUDE

POSITIVELY HEALTHY

POSITIVELY BRAINY

POSITIVE ABOUT PEOPLE

A POSITIVE MOOD

Be active

It's obvious that physical activity is good for our bodies but did you know that it's *very* good for our brains? It's good for our whole mental and physical well-being.

Lots of experts say exercise is the most important part of being healthy, helping us avoid many serious illnesses, feel better in ourselves and generally have a much more positive outlook.

I'll let you know the benefits and then I'll tell you how you can find something that suits you, even if you don't think you want to exercise or don't think you can. There is something for everyone, of whatever ability!

Having said that, before changing your level of exercise significantly you should get medical advice, in case there's a reason why you should avoid certain things.

What good does exercise do?

Different exercise has different benefits. To have an all-round effect, you need a combination of aerobic exercise that makes you a bit out of breath (such as brisk walking, dancing or jogging) and muscle-building exercise or 'resistance' exercise involving pushing and pulling (such as push-ups, sit-ups or using small weights). There are also stretching exercises which protect muscles and make you more flexible.

Exercise has these benefits if you do a variety of different types of exercise:

✱ Strengthens your heart. The heart is a muscle and it gets stronger when it has to work a bit harder some of the time. You shouldn't over-do it, but for most people it's good to raise the heart rate about three times a week.

✱ Increases the amount of oxygen your body can use, by improving how much your lungs can take in.

✱ Protects your joints by building muscles around them. (Over-exercise can damage joints, though, so if you do something a lot it's important to get advice from a sports expert, such as your PE teacher or someone working at the local gym or swimming pool.)

✱ Builds bone strength, so you're less likely to break bones when you're older. For this you need 'weight-bearing' exercise. For example, jogging helps strengthen bones in the legs and using weights builds bones in arms or legs. (Again, doing too much can have the opposite effect: for example, people who jog too much on hard surfaces can get fractures in their shin bones.)

✱ Improves mood. There's masses of evidence about this now and many mental health experts encourage anyone who suffers from mental illness to try to exercise. Any time you're feeling down, a bit of exercise, even going for a quick walk, is likely to have an immediate positive effect.

✱ Improves how your brain works, including things like concentration and focus, as well as memory and planning.

✱ Helps you process what you've just learnt. A number of studies have looked at the effects of learning something and then doing physical exercise and results suggest that physical exercise helps your brain process what you've just learnt, so that you recall it better later.

✱ Helps your brain produce new neurons (those nerve cells that carry messages around your brain and down your spinal cord). Years ago, people thought we didn't make new neurons but now it seems we do and one of the things that can trigger this is physical exercise. Scientists believe this because of studies showing that mice grow neurons when they spend a lot of time going round their wheel.

✱ Helps sleep. It may be partly because exercise improves our mood, and that could help sleep, but there's good evidence that doing exercise earlier in the day does tend to give us better sleep. Don't do energetic exercise in the evening, though: do it earlier in the day and just do gentle stretches or yoga to relax you before bed.

What if you don't like exercise or can't do it?

Some people love being active but others say they don't. And there are lots of obstacles that might make it difficult to get a healthy level of exercise.

One problem is that when we think about exercise we think about getting hot and sweaty, being out of breath, competitive, aggressive, self-conscious or even getting hurt. But 'being active' does not have to involve any of those things! I believe there *is* a physical activity for everyone, something out there that you can enjoy even if you *think* you can't. So, people who 'say' they don't enjoy it are perhaps thinking about the wrong sorts of exercise for them.

Being active can just be going for a walk, bowling, dancing, doing some stretches in your room, walking up and down the stairs. It can be social or it can be solitary. You don't have to join a team or a class if you don't want to. You just have to not sit down too much of the time.

Sitting too much is unhealthy. If you investigate the phrase 'sedentary lifestyle' you'll find lots of research about the health problems associated with sitting for too long. ('Sedentary' literally means 'sitting'.)

I'm a writer so I have to sit for long periods. Or do I? Actually, no. I write standing up. To be accurate, I write while walking on an office treadmill! Obviously, this isn't something you can do at school or even at home, I assume, but it illustrates that there are ways to get exercise even if you have to sit a lot.

EXERCISING WITH A DISABILITY

What about people who *have* to sit: people in wheelchairs, for a start? What happens if you are disabled so that it's difficult or impossible for you to get up and be active? How are you supposed to react to being told to take more exercise?

Well, this message is about doing what you can. Everyone's disability is different but there is always something you can do to raise your heart rate. Not everyone can achieve the amazing results of the Paralympians, just as not every able-bodied person can reach elite levels either – especially me! But what disabled athletes show is that there are many ways of using your body actively, many ways of being *able*, even if you are *dis*abled in some way. Exercising with your arms raises your heart rate, for example. Any physical activity that makes your heart go faster has all the same benefits as for able-bodied people. And whichever parts of your body work well are the ones you can use for exercising. Your doctor or occupational therapist will be happy to help you find something you can do and most local councils offer suitable activities for everybody.

If you have any disability, follow the guidelines for everyone as far as possible and then get extra help from doctors and experts in your specific condition.

How much exercise should you do?

Of course, if you have an illness or disability, check with your doctor in case different guidelines apply. Otherwise, the UK NHS recommends that teenagers should be active for at least an hour every day. But this does not mean you have to do *organised sport* for an hour every day! It just means being as active as you can, rather than sitting still.

Experts also recommend a mixture of three sorts of activity:

* Activity that raises the heart rate. This can be 'moderate', which means that you can talk *as you exercise* but not sing a song. Examples might include fast walking or cycling. Or they can be 'vigorous', which would mean you'd be unable to talk while doing them. Examples might be running, dancing or football.

* Activity that strengthens bones. This is any activity that uses your legs or arms in a way that creates an 'impact' or pressure. So, anything involving running or jumping (for the legs) or weight training, gymnastics or tennis (for arms and legs).

* Activity that strengthens muscles. Most exercise will strengthen some muscles but ideally you want to strengthen lots of muscles so you'll need to think of some different activities. Muscles are especially strengthened when we do things involving lifting our own weight (such as push-ups or pull-ups) or having a resistance against something (such as weights, a ball/racquet).

Some simple and fun examples

Here are some things you might think about trying. Not all of them will be suitable for you so just choose the ones you think might work. And then use your imagination to think of more!

★ With a friend, go to the local park and walk round it several times. Do one minute of fast walking followed by two or three minutes of slow walking.

★ Walk on your own while listening to music. Again, a minute fast walking followed by two or three minutes gentle walking.

★ In your room, dance to your favourite music (with head-phones if you want to!). If you can't use your legs, dance with your arms.

★ Don't use a lift or escalator – use the stairs.

★ Go for a swim.

★ Go online and find exercise workouts that suit you. You'll find some that are free and cater for all ages and abilities.

★ At your local sports centre or at school, join a yoga class or any other class that takes your fancy. Go with a friend if you want to.

★ Walk up and down the stairs in your house several times. Count how many you managed before giving up. See if you can do more tomorrow.

★ Learn how to do a few exercises properly, so you can do them on your own. Your P.E. teacher would be delighted to show you!

★ Plan ahead. Make a chart to remind yourself what to do each day and record what you did.

★ Remember to include all the activity you have to do at school. And even if you don't like it, be as active as possible because it all counts towards your health.

★ Tree-climbing. (I need to say 'be careful' here, but if you've got somewhere you can safely climb it's a very useful activity. *It's great for balance, core stability and strength.* Some adults are going to *criticise* me for suggesting tree-climbing, as it's usually unsupervised and there's a risk of injury. I'm going to trust you to do it carefully with friends with you. Don't be too ambitious and don't go too high. Be positively responsible for your own safety.)

★ Fly a kite.

★ Check out YouTube for some exercise videos appropriate to your age and fitness.

★ Buy an exercise band – a strip of rubber band that allows you to do a load of strength exercises in your own time and in privacy.

★ If you are walking to the shops or to school or the bus-stop, walk faster!

★ Go to your local library and see what classes or activities are advertised.

If you look at **Have a hobby** on page 135, you'll see loads of physical activities that young people do to give you some more ideas.

An important warning: be careful not to exercise too much. If you're an athlete or training for a competition, you will be doing lots of exercise, of course, but you'll have a coach whose job is to make sure you also eat and drink properly and that you are not doing anything likely to give you problems in the future. If you exercise excessively, without expert supervision, you could cause long-term health problems for yourself.

If you exercise, have something healthy to eat and drink afterwards to replace the energy your body has used up.

Exercise is fantastic for a positive lifestyle, but it's possible to have too much. Do enough of it to keep you healthy but not so much that you cause yourself harm, lower your energy levels and develop an unhealthy relationship with exercise. It should be something to enjoy and to make you feel great, rather than something that is a compulsion.

Let exercise be part of being positively teenage.

Resources

HEALTHY EXERCISE

Why be active?

NHS: *http://www.nhs.uk/Livewell/fitness/Pages/whybeactive.aspx*

Kids Health: *http://kidshealth.org/en/teens/exercise-wise.html*

The Brainflux website details many benefits to exercise and links to research for each, including improving willpower, concentration, memory and sleep: *http://thebrainflux.com/brain-benefits-of-exercise/*

How much activity?

The US and UK official guidelines for young people are an hour a day.

US guidelines: *https://health.gov/paguidelines/guidelines/chapter3.aspx*

UK guidelines and ideas: *http://www.nhs.uk/Livewell/fitness/Pages/physical-activity-guidelines-for-young-people.aspx*

World Health Organisation guidelines: *http://www.who.int/dietphysicalactivity/factsheet_young_people/en/*

Research

Mood: *www.ncbi.nlm.nih.gov/pmc/articles/PMC1424736/pdf/pubhealthrep00100-0085.pdf*

Improving higher brain functions, including planning: *www.ncbi.nlm.nih.gov/pubmed/2322944*

Improving concentration: *www.pnas.org/content/101/9/3316.abstract*

Short-term memory: *https://www.ncbi.nlm.nih.gov/pubmed/25304335*

Long-term memory: *www.ncbi.nlm.nih.gov/pmc/articles/PMC2897704/*

An article in the *Guardian* newspaper, on research suggesting that different activities have different effects on your brain: *www.theguardian.com/education/2016/jun/18/how-physical-exercise-makes-your-brain-work-better*

Growing neurons: *www.ncbi.nlm.nih.gov/pmc/articles/PMC1360197/*

A TED talk on this from neuroscientist Sandrine Thuret: *www.ted.com/talks/sandrine_thuret_you_can_grow_new_brain_cells_here_s_how/transcript?language=en*

Helping sleep

The Sleep Foundation: *sleepfoundation.org/sleep-news/study-physical-activity-impacts-overall-quality-sleep*

Too much sitting is unhealthy

Teenagers: *physicalactivityteens.weebly.com/consequences-of-physical-inactivity-in-teenagers.html*

Activity for young people with disabilities

NHS: *www.nhs.uk/change4life/pages/disability-activities-kids.aspx*

Ideas for exercising without going to a gym or playing organised sport:

NHS: *www.nhs.uk/Livewell/fitness/Pages/Getfitwithoutgym.aspx*

Kids Health has yoga-type exercises for short breaks: *kidshealth.org/en/teens/yoga-break.html?WT.ac=ctg#catstudysmart*

Sleep well

Sleep is a weird thing if you think about it. There's such a big and mysterious difference between being conscious, in control and thinking sensibly and being unconscious, out of control and with weird dreams instead of sensible thoughts. What goes on in our brain and body while we sleep? What is sleep *for*? How important is it and what happens if we don't get enough? I'll answer those questions first and then help you know how to fall asleep more quickly and get better sleep.

People used to think sleep was simply for rest and to build up energy. It certainly does that. But we know now there's much more to it.

Thousands of years ago, sleep would have been dangerous: while you were asleep, a predator or enemy could attack you. This applies to all living creatures and each species has evolved its own way to sleep safely. For example, dolphins and whales sleep with one half of their brain asleep at a time. They are 'conscious breathers' and can only breathe when they remember to, whereas we breathe even when unconscious. Some animals go to sleep for the winter, to avoid having to eat when there's not much food. Many animals – such as cats – have lots of short sleeps and are able to snap awake quickly.

The sleep cycle

Humans usually have one long sleep during the hours of darkness, but we aren't in deep sleep all that time. We have five or six cycles of sleep, each one about an hour and a half long. During each cycle, we go through five stages of sleep. And each one is important in different ways.

✳ **Stage one** is a short period of light sleep. If something wakes you during this time, you won't feel groggy and you'll feel you've hardly been asleep.

Lots of creative ideas happen during this stage. Some artists and scientists try to wake themselves up at this point so that they can access their creativity. Scientist Albert Einstein and artist Salvador Dali both did this. Dali used to have a nap with a metal spoon in his hand, dangling over a metal tray. As he relaxed into sleep, the spoon would drop, waking him up with the clatter, and he would write down whatever thoughts were in his head.

✳ **Stage two** is also a fairly light sleep. It lasts about 20 minutes during the early parts of the night but less in later parts of the night. This is a restful stage for your brain and there is little activity in the thinking, learning and problem-solving areas. Scientists believe this is the stage that is most important for strengthening networks for physical skills such as music, gymnastics, other sporting skills or operating devices and tools. Things that you have to learn 'how to do'.

✳ **Stages three** and **four** are much deeper, with your body relaxed and brain activity very slow. If someone tries to wake you they will find it difficult and if something or someone does force you to wake up you feel groggy and disorientated. These deep-sleep stages are important for physical and mental well-being. It's during this time that your body produces growth hormone. This obviously helps you grow at the right speed but is also important for repairing damage to cells. During these stages, your brain repeats things you were focusing on during the day. Suppose you were practising a musical instrument and not managing to play the piece well, or you were shooting basketball nets and becoming frustrated at making mistakes, or you were trying to understand some maths or learn some history: your brain will practise those actions and thought processes and even clear away some of the faulty brain networks. The sleeping brain does a lot of clearing away of dead cells and broken connections during this stage. The spaces between your neurons expand to let more fluid through – a bit like washing the kitchen floor!

You are not dreaming during any of these stages. You may have random thoughts, images or ideas but these are not the sort of things we call dreams, where whole stories happen.

✳ Stage five is the dreaming stage. It's often called REM sleep. REM stands for Rapid Eye Movement because that's what happens when you're in it! If you've ever watched someone in REM sleep you'll see their eyelids twitch. Behind the eyelids their eyes are moving fast.

During this stage, your brain is *very* active, almost as if you're awake, but your body is paralysed, so you don't usually act out your dreams. (Unless you sleepwalk, which is a sleep disorder that is more common in children than adults. It's not usually a problem, but it can be worrying and exhausting. So, if you are doing this you should get advice from a doctor. One of the main causes is sleep deprivation so going to bed earlier could help.)

Scientists are beginning to unlock the mysteries of dreaming, but they still don't know everything. They believe that REM sleep is important to mental health, allowing us to process difficult or traumatic events. It also seems to help us build strong memories and can sometimes help us work out solutions to problems.

How much sleep do you need?

Everyone is a bit different and some differences depend on age. On average, a healthy adult needs about eight hours and a healthy teenager a little over nine. We seem to be able to *manage* on less than that but those figures are good to aim for.

You might be wondering if it's OK to get our sleep in small chunks rather than one long sleep? Well, it's better to do that than not get enough, but it's best to have it in one go. Remember I said that we usually have five or six sleep cycles of roughly one and a half hours? The thing is that although the cycles are roughly the same length, the earlier ones have more light sleep and less deep sleep, whereas the later ones have more deep sleep. So, if you have too little sleep overall, you'll miss some deep sleep. People who work shifts and have irregular or short sleep sessions usually find it has a bad effect on mood and performance.

But we all have times when we can't get enough sleep. When that happens, we mustn't worry about it. We just need to do our best to get back to a healthy level.

What about daytime naps – do they count?

Yes, they can (if you're lucky enough to get the chance!). They can be a really good idea. But try not to sleep for longer than 20 minutes or you'll wake feeling groggy.

What happens when we don't get enough?

At first, nothing. Obviously, you might feel a bit tired the next day. But you definitely shouldn't be stressed about one really bad night's sleep, especially before an exam or something else you're worried about. The chemical adrenalin, from nerves and excitement, will give you the energy you need.

But if you regularly don't have enough sleep, you're likely to notice the following: feeling unwell; not being able to concentrate; making mistakes; not doing your work well at school; low mood; and finding it harder to control your response to anger or other emotions. These things can lead to problems with friendships and affect your school results. It's also likely to affect how well your brain learns.

Just ask yourself this: do you think your school work is as good as it could be? If you think it could be better, maybe getting more sleep would help.

How can you get a good night's sleep?

This is the most important question of all and I have some strategies, based on strong science! And tell your adults because all of this applies to them equally. During the hour or two before you want to feel sleepy, think about the following principles:

✱ Make your brain think it's later at night than it is, by removing daylight from your room. You need thick curtains or blackout blinds. Close them at least an hour and a half before you want to sleep.

✱ Create a routine, to trick your brain into thinking it's bedtime. You can choose a few things to do in the same order each evening before getting into bed and turning the light off. The brain loves a routine and will quickly learn to *recognise* this as your pre-bed routine. (Choose anything from the list of Sleep Positives on page 115.)

✱ Calm your brain and body down. This involves only doing things from the Sleep Positives list and never doing things from the Sleep Negatives list, during the hour and a half before bedtime.

Sleep Positives

✳ Switch off all devices such as TV, computer, phone, tablet

✳ Switch off bright lights and close curtains or blinds

✳ Have a small snack if you're hungry – something milky or carbohydrate-based: a sandwich, for example, or a milky drink and a banana

✳ Tidy your work away and get things ready for the morning

✳ Get undressed ready for bed

✳ Have a bath or shower

✳ Listen to slow, soft music

✳ Do gentle stretching or yoga

✳ Read a book or listen to a podcast.

Sleep Negatives

✳ Bright lights

✳ All screen-based devices

✳ Loud noise

✳ Excitement, anger, stress

✳ Fast exercise

✳ Caffeinated drinks – coffee, ordinary tea and cola, for example

✳ Too much food.

POSITIVELY YOU

A POSITIVE ATTITUDE

POSITIVELY HEALTHY

POSITIVELY BRAINY

POSITIVE ABOUT PEOPLE

A POSITIVE MOOD

★ Create your own sleep routine

Your routine will work so much better if you have chosen it yourself. Here's what to do:

Decide what time you plan to get into bed.

Plan to begin the first item of your routine between 60 and 90 minutes before this.

★ The routine should always include 'Remove daylight from my room'. This means both through the window (with thick curtains or blackout blinds) and from screens. So, your first item should ideally be: finish all screen-based things so I can switch them off.

★ As well as 'remove daylight' and 'switch off screens', choose approximately five items from the list of Sleep Positives. You can also add your own things if you are sure they are good for pre-sleep – ask an adult if you're not sure.

★ 'Get into bed' should obviously be in there! Once in bed, you can read a book or do anything gently relaxing. (No online or mobile-connected activity, of course!)

Write them in a list, in the order you think it would be best to do them.

Start your routine today if it's not too late. Always do the things in the same order. You should notice yourself sleeping more easily after a week or so. If you don't, keep going. It's still a very healthy way to prepare for sleep.

How to get to sleep when it feels impossible

This is something almost everyone experiences. Often it's when a worry goes round and round our mind. Sometimes it's when we're really excited and can't calm down. And sometimes it's when we are over-stimulated by lights, noise, screens, or unusual things that happened during the day.

Here's the best advice:

✳ Stop thinking about sleep. Stop even trying to sleep. It doesn't matter right now.

✳ If the cause is a worry, write it on a piece of paper. Then fold the paper several times and put it by the door. Tell yourself there's nothing more you can do about it and you'll sort it tomorrow if possible. If that isn't possible, thinking about it won't help.

✳ Sort out anything that's making you uncomfortable: needing the toilet, being too cold/hot, wrinkly sheets and duvet.

✳ Slow your breathing a little. Focus on it. Count slow breaths until you feel calmer – do it for several minutes, if you like.

✳ Now, *visualise* your perfect place. It can be somewhere you've been or somewhere in your imagination. Build up the detail. Where are you: garden, beach, bed, holiday, alone or with friends? What can you see: colours, trees, beach, sea, clouds, birds? What can you smell: suncream, cake, sea, scented candles? What can you hear: waves, cars, people, wind, nothing? How do you feel: warm, peaceful, relaxed, unbothered? Think of your fingers, toes, stomach, the skin on your face. If any bad thoughts come in, just let them go and focus back on what you want to think about.

Don't fret if it doesn't work quickly. It's good that you're resting and relaxed. Try not to think about getting to sleep: just focus on whatever positive thoughts you like. If you can't get to sleep for a while, you can choose either to carry on lying there, resting, breathing slowly, or you can read a book or listen to very soft music. Don't be tempted to turn your phone or other Internet-enabled device on.

Sleep is a really important part of looking after yourself. It might feel like something you can't control and to *some* extent that's true, at least sometimes. But there are things you can do that will help. You have the tools now. When you really *can't* sleep, don't stress about it.

I have to say this one more time because it's the most important thing for a good night's sleep, for adults too: switch off all digital devices well before bedtime. It will help, trust me!

Resources

SLEEP

Getting better sleep

From Kids Health: *kidshealth.org/en/teens/tips-sleep.html?WT.ac=p-ra*

From the NHS, aimed at parents: *www.nhs.uk/Livewell/Childrenssleep/Pages/teensleeptips.aspx*

From Young Minds, aimed at teenagers, includes sections on nightmares and bad dreams: *youngminds.org.uk/find-help/feelings-and-symptoms/sleep-problems/*

Effects of sleep on memory/learning

From Harvard University: *healthysleep.med.harvard.edu/healthy/matters/benefits-of-sleep/learning-memory*

While you're asleep, rubbish in your brain is cleaned up!

From the National Institute of Health: *https://www.nih.gov/news-events/nih-research-matters/how-sleep-clears-brain*

Sleepwalking

From the Sleep Foundation: *sleepfoundation.org/sleep-disorders-problems/abnormal-sleep-behaviors/sleepwalking/page/0/1*

Summing up

In this section, you've learnt so many practical ways to look after your well-being and be healthy. You know how to make sure you're eating enough and I've given you loads of options when it comes to eating the right types of food to make you healthy.

You've learnt about the importance of drinking enough water, getting sunlight on your skin and you've found out how to breathe properly to help concentration and mood.

You've discovered the importance of taking exercise for the health of your body and also your brain. You've found out how important sleep is to your well-being and how to get a good night's sleep.

There is so much you can do to keep control and have a brilliantly positive effect on your own life and health. Your body and brain will thank you!

Positively Brainy

Your brain is amazing! It's responsible for everything you can do and everything you feel and think. It's your control centre and in it are all your memories and everything that you know, as well as the keys to your personality. But your brain is not fixed: it's changing all the time. Everything you do makes a difference to your brain, setting down a physical pathway that makes that thing easier the next time. Scientists don't yet know everything about the human brain but we know much more than we did when your parents were children. And one thing we know is that there are things we can do to make our brains work better for us, so that we can have the best control over our lives and our success. That's what this section is about.

All the other things in this book – eating well, sleeping, exercising, being social, having a positive attitude – they all help, too. But this section focuses on some very particular things that directly affect how your brain works.

Are you ready to become positively brainy?

Practice makes perfect

People have probably been saying that for hundreds of years but you might have noticed that it's not always true! It's often not possible to become 'perfect'. You could become perfect at spelling the word 'immediately' but you couldn't be perfect at swimming or football or maths; or perfect at kindness or at knowing what to say to a friend who's upset. You could try to become perfect at gymnastics or singing, but I think even the world's best gymnasts or singers probably want to be even better than they are.

But practice *does* make us better at whatever we are trying to become better at. And this practice does something particular in our brains.

What I'm about to say now is perhaps the most important thing to know about how the brain works. Knowing this will give you power and a positive attitude to anything you might want to become good at. Are you ready?

How the brain learns

I talked about this in a different way in the introduction to A POSITIVE ATTITUDE on page 46. There, I was talking about how the brain makes pathways for positive and negative thoughts, by repeating the thoughts. So, what I'm about to say about how the brain learns will feel familiar.

When we do something – move a finger, speak, remember the capital of Spain – electrical messages have to pass along correct pathways between neurons. We are born with 85 to 100 billion neurons.

When we're born, most of these neurons aren't connected into pathways, so electrical signals can't travel, so newborn babies can't do much. Also, when we start to learn a new skill at any age, the neurons we'll need haven't formed strong pathways, which is why the first time we try something it's usually difficult.

So, if we want to become good at something, we have to grow connections between the right neurons, so that strong pathways form and the electrical signals can travel easily. The connections are like branches (called dendrites, which is from the Ancient Greek word for 'tree') which reach out and *almost* touch the next neuron. The place where they almost touch is called a synapse and the space is so tiny that the electrical signals can jump across.

Growing these connections is easy! Here's how we do it:

By watching someone else do it. When we watch someone, our own brain activates neurons called mirror neurons, which start imitating the person we are watching. Then, when we try the thing ourselves, it's a bit easier because our brain has actually already started practising, so pathways have begun to form.

By trying – even if we fail. Every time we try to do something, we physically build connections. The more we try, the more connections grow and the stronger they become. This is how practising makes us better: because we are physically building connections and pathways in our brain.

By sleeping! You learnt about this on page 112. Sleep is crucial for learning. You may remember that during certain stages of sleep, your brain 'practises' the things you were trying to do during the day. Your brain is practising for you, while you're asleep. (I did say your brain was amazing!)

The big point is that every time our brain repeats something, it creates a stronger pathway, making it easier next time. If you're finding something difficult, remember that each time you practise, you *are* getting better. Sometimes the improvement is too small to notice, but it all adds up. Remember 'growth mindset'? We become good at things by trying and doing.

Practice might not make perfect, but it does make it better.

But what if you keep repeating a mistake? What if you don't know how to do it and need some help? Let's take a look at how to practise *well*.

Good practising

SPACED LEARNING

If we want to learn something well and remember it for a long time, it's best to learn it in several separate sessions rather than try to learn it all at once. Back in 1885, Hermann Ebbinghaus discovered what he called the 'forgetting curve', showing how we forget over time, and then he found ways to prevent this happening. He discovered that if we repeat our learning with increasing spaces between each session, it goes strongly into our long-term memory and is hard to forget. It's called spaced repetition or spaced learning.

This works especially well for learning vocabulary or dates or facts.

⭐ Let's test the theory!

I'm going to give you two verses of a poem to remember. You can use whatever methods you like: writing or speaking or decorating with colours or whatever you want, but you should use the same method for each.

When you learn the first verse, do this: spend seven minutes learning it now; then spend seven minutes learning it tomorrow; then six minutes two days after that (20 minutes spaced into three sessions).

When you learn the second verse, do this: spend 20 minutes learning it in one go today. Do not look at it again (20 minutes not spaced out at all).

Five days from now, see if you can recite the verses without looking. Which one did you find easier?

Verse 1

He thought he saw an Elephant
That practised on a fife:
He looked again, and found it was
A letter from his wife.

'At length I realise,' he said,
'The bitterness of life!'

Verse 2

He thought he saw a Buffalo
Upon the chimney-piece:
He looked again, and found it was
His Sister's Husband's Niece.

'Unless you leave this house,' he said,
'I'll send for the police!'

(First two verses of 'A Strange Wild Song' by Lewis Carroll)

TAKING BREAKS

There are two reasons why taking breaks is good and why they help you learn. First, you sometimes do need a rest. Studying is tiring! That's not surprising because your brain uses energy.

Secondly, it seems that taking a break to do something different helps the information go into the right parts of the brain. So, if you're trying to learn or understand something, while you take a break your brain continues to process the information, so when you come back to it you've learnt it a bit better.

The best things to do in the breaks are:

* Physical exercise – even just a quick walk outside

* Social activity – face-to-face, not on screen

* Sleep – not more than 20 minutes, though.

Is it better to take a break after finishing a piece of work or before finishing? Research suggests that it is probably better to do it *before*! It's as though unfinished tasks hang around in the memory – a bit like leaving a page open on your computer ready to come back to quickly. It also seems that the best time to interrupt your task with a break is when you're concentrating on it most! When you take a break, your brain carries on mulling things over, even if you aren't thinking about them.

So, take short breaks and go and do something completely different for a few minutes. Your brain will thank you for it.

ASKING FOR HELP

Teachers are there to help you and they *want* to. If you're stuck on something or you're finding a particular activity really hard, ask for help. Don't ask before you've tried, though; have a go first. But don't wait too long, either. It may be that you're just looking at something in the wrong way.

LEARNING STYLES

There was a fashion a few years ago for analysing people's learning styles, to see whether they were 'visual learners', who learn better using their eyes; 'auditory learners' who learn better using their ears; or 'kinaesthetic learners' who learn better using their hands and via practical activities. It's true that you might find one or two of these methods more helpful but they are not fixed aspects of how you are. Most people learn better with a combination of these methods. Practise in a way that suits you. Here are some suggestions you might try:

* Write in a variety of different coloured-pens

* Create pictures or posters to help you remember

* Speak things aloud

* Record what you want to learn and play it back

* Walk while reciting the things you want to learn.

RE-WRITING AND SELF-TESTING

Re-writing and self-testing work particularly well, especially for things you've been reading and trying to understand. Some people make two mistakes when trying to understand and learn written material: they just read it over and over again, without taking it in properly; and they underline or highlight what they think are key points. These things don't usually work well! It's much better to re-write and self-test.

Re-writing means putting something into your own words. The act of doing this helps you understand and remember because it's being processed by more parts of your brain than if you're simply reading over and over. If you also keep asking yourself questions (self-testing) you should find this works even better. So, as you're reading something difficult, ask yourself a question and then answer it in your own words.

For example, suppose you're reading something about the causes of the American Civil War or how the tides work, imagine someone is going to ask you to explain it to them. Have that in mind while you're reading, and then write your answer. Does it make sense? Check back and see if you got it right. All of these steps make it more likely that the information will go properly into your brain as understanding, not just words on a page.

What if you've been practising something wrong?

Just as practising improves skills or knowledge by building pathways in the brain, it's also possible to create the wrong pathway by accidentally practising something that's not correct. Suppose you hadn't been taught how to hold a tennis racquet or you picked up a violin and started trying to play it without lessons: you'd probably be doing it wrong. And the more times you did it wrong the stronger these wrong pathways would become.

So, what's the answer? Get someone to teach you the correct way and keep practising, practising, practising! Soon you'll create the correct pathway and the faulty one will become weaker and weaker. Simple!

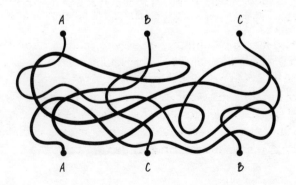

POSITIVELY YOU

A POSITIVE ATTITUDE

POSITIVELY HEALTHY

POSITIVELY BRAINY

POSITIVE ABOUT PEOPLE

A POSITIVE MOOD

POSITIVE BOOST

Using a dictionary (online or print, but print might be easier), choose three fantastic words that you've never heard before. Learn how to spell them and what they mean. See if you can use them in your writing and speech over the next three days!

Research

PRACTICE AND LEARNING

How the brain learns
A simple video: *www.youtube.com/watch?v=uqGz7uqoPZ4*

Spaced learning
There's detail about Hermann Ebbinghaus and the 'forgetting curve' here: *www.growthengineering.co.uk/what-is-the-forgetting-curve/ knowledgeplus.nejm.org/blog/spaced-repetition-the-most-effective-way-to-learn/*

Interrupted tasks
Why taking breaks before you've finished a task may be better than waiting until you've finished, according to Bluma Zeigarnik: *www.psychologistworld.com/memory/zeigarnik-effect-interruptions-memory*

Use lots of areas of your brain

Each different sort of thing you do uses different areas of your brain. If we could put you in a brain-scanning machine called an MRI scanner and ask you to do different activities – such as counting, reading, aiming, singing, recognising faces or imagining the colour red – we would see different combinations of areas of your brain being active. If they are active, they are making and using connections.

If you spend a *lot* of time on one activity, you will grow more and stronger connections in the brain areas that activity uses. To become brilliant at something – football, say, or playing the piano, or drawing faces – you need to grow as many strong connections as possible in the areas you need.

But there's another side to this: the areas you *don't* use much tend to *lose* connections or not grow them in the first place. So you won't have those skills. If you learn a skill and then lose connections later, it's usually not too hard to grow them again. If you never had the skill in the first place, you can *usually* develop it later, but it's much harder.

Here's an example: supposing there's a girl and a boy. It doesn't matter which is which, but supposing the girl learnt Italian well when she was very young because her grandpa was Italian and he taught her. But the boy never learnt Italian. And then supposing the girl's grandpa dies when the girl is about seven and she stops speaking Italian because her parents don't speak it. So, she had built up loads of connections in her brain for speaking Italian but now she loses lots of those connections because she doesn't keep using them.

Then, years later, when the girl and boy are adults, they both decide to learn Italian. The girl will find it easier than the boy because she still has many of those connections left, so she can more easily build them up again.

So, it's good to do loads of different things now, while you're young, to give yourself the best chance to develop the skills you want later. It doesn't matter if you stop after a few years: you've still built important strengths that won't vanish completely.

You can't spend masses of time on *everything* because there are only a certain number of hours in the day, but you can make sure you do a wide variety of activities. Do things you enjoy – because you'll probably do better at them – but also challenge yourself. You can do it!

★ Using your brain

In your *Positively Teenage* notebook, find a clean page and put today's date at the top. Then divide the page into the following sections. (I'm assuming it's a school day; if not, you can either wait till the next school day or adjust it to work for a holiday or weekend.)

Before breaktime

During breaktime

Break until lunch

During lunchtime

Afternoon until end of school

On the way home from school

First part of the evening

Last part of the evening.

Beneath each one, write what you did. At the end of the day, look at your activities. Were there lots of different sorts? Do you think you used lots of brain areas? Which of these were represented?

Physical activity

Music – listening or playing

Art, crafts or making things

Talking

Reading

Writing

Numbers

Puzzles – general knowledge or problem-solving

Hobbies and relaxation

Speaking, reading or listening to a foreign language

Something else I'm good at

Something else I find difficult

Working in a team

Thinking

Daydreaming

Using a screen

Resisting temptation.

What could you add tomorrow to make sure you use lots of brain areas?

Try new things - or do old things differently

When we try new things, our brain wakes up. Remember that chemical called dopamine? (I mentioned it when I talked about the 'I for Interest' part of FLOURISH on page 10.) I called it the 'Yes' chemical and one of the things it says 'Yes' to is anything new. This is an important human behaviour: curiosity. If we are curious about things, we want to discover, explore, know answers. We are likely to find the answers and learn more. Being curious is a sign of intelligence and leads to all sorts of positive things.

To encourage us to be curious, our brains give us a little buzz of excitement (dopamine again) when we experience new things. Cultivate your curiosity! It could give you a burst of energy, a new way of seeing a problem, extra positivity and exciting opportunities that you won't have if you keep your eyes closed.

Some ideas

Can you think of anything you'd like to try but never got round to? What's stopping you? Investigate it and see if you could have a go.

✳ Eat something you've never eaten. Try something strongly flavoured like an olive, or wasabi (careful – it's hot!), fresh coriander, lime juice, Vegemite. Even if you don't like the taste, think about it properly and try to describe it.

✳ Cook something you've never cooked before. If you've never cooked at all, do it! It's fun, easy, useful and healthy. It not only helps inspire you while you're doing it but it's a useful life skill. Start either by looking in the kitchen cupboards or fridge (ask your parents before taking something that might be ready for tonight's dinner!) or grab a recipe book or visit a website for inspiration. It must be something you've never cooked, such as vegan meringues using the water from a can of chickpeas! (Internet search for how to do this – you'll be amazed.)

✳ Challenge yourself to talk to a teacher you've never talked to at school. Ask them what book they are reading. If they aren't reading one, ask them why not.

✳ Ask if you can have a family outing somewhere you've never been.

✳ Go to an art gallery and pretend you're a judge for an art prize. Buy a postcard of the one you decide is the best.

✳ Go to a museum and find out three facts you didn't know. Write them in your notebook.

✳ Pretend you're a tourist in the place where you live. Look at things through a tourist's eyes.

* Learn to say 'hello', 'goodbye', 'please', 'thank you' and 'caterpillar' (or any random word you'd like to know) in a new language.

* If you're over 12, maybe you could ask a generous relative to pay for a young driver's lesson! Or save up yourself. See if there's an organisation near you that offers this.

Look at the list of hobbies (on pages 136–140) and choose one you've never tried.

Some ideas for doing old things differently

* Rearrange the furniture in your room

* Clean your teeth with the hand you don't normally use

* Fold your arms in the normal way and then fold them with the opposite one on top

* Try drawing a picture or writing with your 'wrong' hand

* Walk a different way to school or get on the bus at a different stop

* Do your hair differently

* Speak backwards.

Have a hobby

There are loads of positive reasons to have a hobby. They give you a break from normal school work; help take your mind off worries; develop new skills; exercise different parts of your brain; help you make new friends; and some hobbies even make money. They make us into more rounded, complete people, with a good balance in our lives. They can take your life in interesting new directions and you just never know what might happen. Also, you don't have to do exams or tests in them (though sometimes you can) and if you don't enjoy your hobby you can just stop! What's not to like?!

When I was writing this book, I went onto my social media networks and asked a simple question to my friends who are parents: 'What hobbies do your teenagers have?' I was astonished by the range of answers! I'm going to include them all here, for two reasons: first, so that you can have ideas that you might not have thought of (though some are more obvious). Second, because I want adults to stop saying, 'Oh, teenagers – they just spend all their time on the Internet'.

POSITIVELY YOU

A POSITIVE ATTITUDE

POSITIVELY HEALTHY

POSITIVELY BRAINY

POSITIVE ABOUT PEOPLE

A POSITIVE MOOD

I've tried to divide them into categories but there's an overlap so don't take too much notice of that. On YouTube you'll find videos to show you how to do whatever you're interested in.

Physical activities that usually need lessons or coaching and are mostly done in groups, teams or clubs:

Swimming – competitively or just for health

Diving

Scuba-diving

Ice hockey

Hockey

Rugby

Football refereeing! (You can earn money doing this, apparently.)

Ballet

Street dance or break dancing

Scottish/Highland/country dancing

Indian dancing – and other international dancing

Guides and Scouts – various organisations for different ages around the world

Geocaching – great family activity

Orienteering

Gymnastics

Trampolining

Fencing – this is also great for people with dyspraxia, because you're not using both sides of your body in the same way at the same time. Several people mentioned that it's great for those who find social situations difficult – the mask helps!

Martial arts

Circus school and aerial skills, such as silks, hoops and dance

Bell ringing

Canoeing and rowing

Sailing

Skiing and snowboarding

Archery

Combined Cadet Force (or other army or navy cadets) – develops fantastic skills, such as teamwork and managing people.

Physical activities that may require lessons/coaching but can often be done solo or with friends:

Climbing (indoor climbing centre) – this was mentioned as especially suiting people who like to work on their own, not in groups

Parkour

BMX and other biking

Dog-training

Stunt scooting

Skateboarding

Go-karting

Horse riding – if you help out at the stables this cuts the cost

Golf

Football

Cricket

Skating

POSITIVELY YOU

A POSITIVE ATTITUDE

POSITIVELY HEALTHY

POSITIVELY BRAINY

POSITIVE ABOUT PEOPLE

A POSITIVE MOOD

Bike riding

Going for walks

Bird-watching.

Mental activities:

Reading – on your own or
in book groups at school, library or online

Computer coding

Electronics and robotics

Computer gaming – if it doesn't become an obsession which
occupies an unhealthy amount of time. 'Unhealthy' would
be an amount of time that prevents you from having enough
physical and face-to-face social activity and doing your work

Solving Rubik Cubes

Puzzles, such as Sudoku

Science clubs

Bridge and other card games

Watching films and learning all the facts behind them

Becoming an expert – your chosen topic could be your
favourite band or celebrity, all the capital cities around the
world, someone from history, dinosaurs, your favourite author,
anything.

Creative activities:

Writing – either on your own or at a club, library or school – maybe using Wattpad. You could write a private journal; or a blog, which can be private or for a wider audience – ask your school librarian or teacher for advice about staying safe with this; or writing stories and poems, either just for fun or aiming to be a published writer one day.

Art

Making Manga comics

Animation and movie making, including stop-animation

Photography

Playing musical instruments for orchestra or solo playing

Steel pan drums – I know this is part of the previous point, but I felt it deserved a mention!

Singing

Composing songs

Drama – either acting or back stage, on stage management or lighting or whatever

Baking and other cooking; sushi-making; chocolate-making

Sewing

Knitting, crochet, finger-knitting

Basket-making from local materials

Origami

Crafts; model-making from kits

Woodwork

Tie-dyeing

Pottery

Glass painting.

Things that can be 'hobbies' or just good ways of passing the time and using different areas of the brain:

All the above ideas can obviously also work like this, too – you don't have to have actual 'hobbies', just things you enjoy doing.

Nature and ecology, bugs and birds

Rummaging in the woods, making bows and arrows and carving things out of dead wood

Climbing trees

Gardening – this was mentioned several times. You don't need a big garden. In fact, you don't need a garden at all. There are loads of things that can be grown in a pot on a windowsill, depending on where you live.

Bonsai – something to grow that doesn't need much space at all

Sunday school or other cultural club

Young Farmers groups

Fixing bikes and learning how machines work

Upcycling – turning used items into something else and selling or using them

Making beauty treatments

Volunteering for all sorts of charities, befriending the elderly

Collecting things – anything: egg cups, ponies (model ones…), shells, wild flowers (don't dig anything up), coins, stamps, photos of sports stars.

If you don't think those ideas are interesting enough, I was told about some more that were slightly too unusual to put in the main list: competitive sheep-shearing; competitive wood chopping; breeding sheep, alpaca and angora rabbits; and sheepdog training! Those were from rural Australia, but you probably have some local activities and crafts where you are.

I hope adults are impressed by this. I'm exhausted. Go, positively teenagers!

Control your screen use

Our screen-based devices such as laptops, tablets and smartphones are amazing and powerful. They give us huge possibilities to find out about anything in the world and to connect with other people of all types. Those are really important benefits, that make your generation often so much broad-minded and knowledgeable than I was at your age. But there may be some problems from using screens too much – and many of us do use screens a lot and sometimes too much.

Let's take a quick look at the possible problems and then think how we can use our screens healthily and positively.

First, did you notice that I said 'we'? That's because what I'm about to say applies equally to me and all the adults you know, as well as you! Tell your parents that if you have to be careful about screen use, so do they, for exactly the same reasons. To be honest, I am quite unimpressed by the way some adults use their screens while telling you not to. When it's unhealthy for you, it's unhealthy for them. And they should set a good example.

DISTRACTION

Screens of all sorts (especially if connected to the Internet or other people) are distracting and the science is clear on this. Research shows that even if someone next to us is on a laptop and we're not, we are usually slightly distracted by it. (The loss of concentration is measurable and can make us perform less well on a task.) Just having our phone in sight occupies a tiny bit of concentration so we focus less well on the task we're trying to do. And some studies suggest that if we read information on a screen we comprehend and process the information less well and remember it less well than if we read it on paper. (The difference is only small but we should think about it. This seems to apply to all age groups, not just older people who didn't grow up with this technology.)

One problem is that our screens bring lots of temptations: icons, adverts and links encouraging us to click on them. Our curious minds notice these distractions and we spend a lot of brainpower deciding which to ignore and which to follow. There's a *lot* of evidence that this is all making many people less good at concentrating for a long period of time. I'm afraid there's also evidence that your age group is more distractible than teenagers used to be, even though you grew up with everything digital.

Screens usually force us to multi-task and almost no one is good at that. We might think we are but we can't really do well on a high-concentration task if something else is occupying some of our brain 'bandwidth'. It's like trying to do something on a broadband line that is being used by someone streaming some video or television. Everything slows down and it doesn't work so well.

★ Quiz

You can find more detailed quizzes online but this is a good start to discover whether you may have an unhealthy Internet use. For each of these questions, answer: Never, Almost Never, Sometimes, Quite Often or Very Often. These questions refer to social and pleasure use, when you use your screen-based device for personal, not work, reasons. And 'online' includes anything you do on your mobile phone, Internet or computer game device.

★ How often do you find you've been online for longer than you intended?

★ How often do you find you haven't got enough time for your school work because you've been online?

★ When you're not online, are you thinking about the next time you can go online?

★ How often do you check your notifications (from any social media, email or gaming community etc) before you start your homework?

★ Are you sometimes secretive about how much time you spend online?

★ Do you feel happier when you're online than when you're offline?

★ Do you pick up your smartphone to avoid talking to people?

Score as follows:

Never = 0; Almost Never = 1; Sometimes = 2; Quite Often = 3; Very Often = 4

Your score:

First, note that if you scored 3 or 4 on *any* questions, this should encourage you to change your behaviour in this area.

0-7 You don't have a real problem with your screen use. (But see my point above.)

8-14 This is an acceptable score, though 13/14 are borderline. And, as above, a 3 or 4 score on any answer should alert you to take more care.

15+ It's definitely worth finding ways to moderate your use, for the sake of your health, well-being and work.

19+ It's very likely that you are using your devices in a potentially unhealthy way and you'd feel and function better if you were able to stay offline more.

ADDICTION

These devices have some addictive aspects, in similar ways to such things as sugar, tobacco, alcohol and illegal drugs. This does *not* mean everyone will become addicted or that the addiction would be as dangerous as the others I mentioned. But it's so easy to find that we want to go online or play screen-based games more and more and more. If this means we aren't spending enough time on other things – such as school work, getting outside for fresh air, and chatting with family and friends – that's a problem.

LOSING SKILLS?

Most of us have gained lots of skills and important knowledge through the Internet. But we may also be losing some. Some people worry that our memory is getting worse because we don't usually need to remember things, now that we can so easily look anything up. I'm not sure, and I'm not even sure it matters, if it means we can do other things with our brains. The ancient Greeks worried that if people had things written down they'd lose their memory, too, but we still seem to have pretty good brains.

There's one thing I do worry some people are losing: the skill of talking. Making conversation is often hard; it needs practice and effort. But so often we just pull out a phone instead of talking to people. If I ruled the world, people would never have their phones on or visible while having a meal or spending time with someone. I love my phone and I am guilty of using it too much, but real people come first.

Teenagers often tell me how annoying and upsetting it is when parents use phones when their teenagers want to talk to them. Unless it's a complete emergency, which it hardly ever is, that's not acceptable. You have my permission to tell them off!

So, do keep talking to people. It's a really important skill for getting on in life, useful socially and for your careers. It's a fundamental human behaviour and one that has contributed to our success. And it does need practice. If you avoid talking because it's so much easier to use your phone, you'll find it harder when you need to talk. You'll find ideas to help with this in POSITIVE ABOUT PEOPLE on page 151.

LOSING THINKING TIME

Any time we have five minutes waiting for a bus, many of us don't spend those minutes thinking or looking at the sky or trees: we get our phone out and check to see how many 'likes' our latest social media post had. Of course that doesn't matter sometimes, but if it means we don't get any time just to ripple through our thoughts, I think that's an important loss.

I will talk about this much more in **Just think** on page 196.

A healthy balance

As I say, there's nothing wrong with screens. but it becomes a problem when we use them too much. If we do, we must be missing out on other important things. It's the same with video games: there's nothing wrong with them, until we do them so much that we negatively affect our other activities or find it really hard to stop.

Somehow, we need to find a balance. There's no rule about how much or how little screen time is OK, but it has to be an amount that *feels* right and that allows us to do lots of other things, too.

Think about whether your screen use stops you doing any of these things:

✳ Work – school work, homework, whatever

✳ Friends – you might engage with friends on social media but that isn't enough. Even quiet people benefit from seeing other people. (I'll talk about that in the next section.)

* Physical exercise and fresh air

* Eating and sleeping

* Hobbies and interests – some of this might be online; that's fine but see the next point

* Being offline!

Some ideas

SWITCH OFF SCREEN (SOS) TIME

This should be the whole family; it can also work well at school and if your school has SOS time, embrace this. You might moan about it with your friends, but if you're all doing it, it's easy! Notice how good it feels to be offline for a while. At family meal times, actually talk to each other about your day, ask questions, get cross about something you heard in the news, discuss your next holiday or what you want to do at the weekend.

OUT OF SIGHT, OUT OF MIND

When you're working, make sure your phone is out of sight. Ideally not in the same room. If it has to be in the room, have it completely switched off and in your bag.

APPS

There are apps to help avoid the temptation of checking social media while working. You can set them so that they block just social media, email or the whole Internet. I won't name any, as they keep changing, but you should be able to find a free one. Use it! You'll feel good and you'll get your work done so much faster and better.

POSITIVELY YOU

A POSITIVE ATTITUDE

POSITIVELY HEALTHY

POSITIVELY BRAINY

POSITIVE ABOUT PEOPLE

A POSITIVE MOOD

POMODORO TECHNIQUE

Do an Internet search for this technique for time management, based on the simple idea of a kitchen timer. You can use a timer or a Pomodoro app. You choose an amount of time – 25 minutes is good because it doesn't feel too long – set the timer, switch off or block social media, and work well for that amount of time. The amazing thing is that when the timer pings you usually want to carry on working! I know it sounds unbelievable but it seems to let you get into the zone and the feeling of working well is so good that you want to do it again.

IF/THEN STRATEGIES

This is a technique used to help people resist temptation. It's very simple, but very effective. You give yourself a rule, like this: 'IF I am tempted to check my Instagram feed, THEN I will drink a sip of water instead.' You probably think I'm weird to suggest something so simple but why not try it? There's good science behind it. It doesn't have to be a glass of water, but anything instead of the thing you want to resist. The good thing about a sip of water is that it's good for you too. Double win!

POSITIVE BOOST

Switch off all screens now and see how you feel. If you've already done it, great! Notice the calm around you and the peace in your head. Notice the absence of that buzzing noise or the lights. Appreciate that for a little while no one can bother you or ask you anything. And you can switch it back on whenever you want, but for now just be chilled and calm.

If you're wondering why I know so many of these strategies, it's because I, too, am very easily tempted to mess around on social media instead of working. So, I have armed myself with all these techniques. They really help!

Resources

CONTROLLING SCREEN USE

Distraction

Teen Ink: www.teenink.com/hot_topics/what_matters/article/781313/Digital-Distraction/

The New York Times on digital distraction: www.nytimes.com/2010/06/07/technology/07brain.html

Time magazine: time.com/money/3956968/cell-phone-alert-productivity/

Distraction from the laptop of the person next to you: www.rcinet.ca/en/2013/08/20/new-study-shows-computers-in-class-distract-both-users-and-non-users/

Having your phone in sight makes you focus less well on the task you're trying to do: psycnet.apa.org/index.cfm?fa=buy.optionToBuy&id=2014-52302-001

And: psmag.com/social-justice/presence-smart-phone-lowers-quality-person-conversations-85805

Digital natives seem not to be better at multi-tasking or dealing with distraction: phys.org/news/2016-01-digital-distraction-class.html

Reading on a digital device may make us comprehend, process and remember less well than if we read it on paper: www.scientificamerican.com/article/reading-paper-screens/

Resisting temptation

Ideas to help us all manage our screen time well:

For parents: healthykidshealthyfuture.org/5-healthy-goals/reduce-screen-time/resources/

From the BBC: www.bbc.com/future/story/20131010-lose-the-phone-reclaim-your-life

You will notice that all the resources above involve using a screen and the Internet! I'm not saying there is anything wrong with *good* use of screens. You might also be interested in my book, *The Teenage Guide to Life Online*, which goes into all this in much more detail.

POSITIVELY YOU

A POSITIVE ATTITUDE

POSITIVELY HEALTHY

POSITIVELY BRAINY

POSITIVE ABOUT PEOPLE

A POSITIVE MOOD

Summing up

In this chapter, you've learnt how practice makes you better at things and what happens in your brain when you do that. You've seen how doing lots of different things will help grow different areas of your brain and you've seen why trying new things and having hobbies creates variety and interest, making your brain more healthy. Finally, you've discovered the benefit of controlling your screen use.

You have so much power, so much potential, the possibility to control so much more than you might think: grow your brain positively and it will repay you with success and confidence.

Positive about People

Humans are social creatures. We need friends and people to support us. Ever since humans existed, we've tended to work in pairs and groups. We have partners, families, friends, communities, clubs, all sorts of groups at school, work and socially. Some of us like spending a lot of time with people and enjoy big groups. Some love spending time on our own, or with just one friend at a time. Often, which of these things we prefer depends on how we are feeling – and who the other people are!

People who enjoy time on their own – and I'm one of them – still need friends. We need to know who we can turn to when we need help or we fancy being with someone else. Psychologists know that networks and friendships are vital to well-being. Not having anyone to turn to is a horrible feeling.

Sometimes, it's easy to make friends. Other times it's harder. But friendships don't happen without us making an effort. A stranger won't turn up on the doorstep and say, 'Will you be my friend?'. (That would be a bit weird!) There are things we need to do to build bonds with people. So, to boost this part of your well-being, there are a few things to do.

Talk
face-to-face

Because of modern technology, we can so easily 'talk' to people online now, but face-to-face is still important, for two main reasons.

First, it helps us build the friendships and support we need or might need one day. Although we can start or continue a friendship online, with texts, social media or other messages, there are advantages when we can see the other person and read their body language and facial expressions. It's easier to know what the other person is really thinking. Talking face-to-face keeps us connected to reality and stops us living too much inside our own heads. (Spending time there is fine as long as we don't hide there excessively!)

Second, talking to people face-to-face is a set of skills we'll need often during our lives, which we need to practise. The ability to talk to someone we don't know is incredibly powerful and opens doors, leading to new experiences, knowledge, opportunities. So many jobs need people who can get on with others.

Here are some examples of when the skill of talking to people will help you:

✳ In an interview

✳ In any job – especially working with people, and that's most jobs

✳ When you want to persuade people of your point of view

✳ When you move somewhere new – new school, job or location

✳ When you have to walk into a room of strangers

✳ When you want to help a friend

✳ When you are trying to sort out problems between people

✳ When you want to be selected for something, such as a team or a play. If you've already engaged with someone by talking to them, they are more likely to pick you or notice you.

But it can be difficult to talk to people, can't it? It's so easy to send a quick text message or communicate through social media. And it's fine to do that sometimes: you're allowed to be on your own and have peace and quiet, some 'me-time'. I'm definitely someone who loves and needs to spend enough time alone. I'm an introvert so, although I manage very well and even enjoy social things, I get tired and stressed if I spend too much time with other people, even people I like.

I believe that making time to talk face-to-face to people gives us a more positive life. And it gets easier with practice. If you give yourself lots of opportunities to talk to people – of your own age and others – you'll grow wonderful skills that will help you throughout your life. You don't have to do anything special or difficult: just don't *avoid* face-to-face situations. Join in conversations when you can and don't worry if you sometimes can't think of anything to say: listening is just as important in conversation as talking is. In fact, the world would be a better place if people spent more time listening!

It's perfectly OK to be a quiet or shy person. These are not problems. But they do mean you might need to try extra hard and make sure you don't hide behind your smartphone. Be proud every time you join in a conversation and realise that you're doing yourself some good. Gradually, it will get easier and you'll learn to act more confidently.

Ideas for starting conversations

* Ask a question. 'Where did you get your jacket?' 'What do you think of the geography teacher?' 'Did you watch *The X-Factor*?'

* Make eye contact – actual eye contact, not a quick glance at their forehead. Just for a few seconds – anything more is staring! This can be incredibly hard for some people and you might have to force yourself, but I promise it will get easier. Practise on your family.

* Simple situations like buying something in a shop or ordering a drink can give opportunities to use eye contact, a smile and a few words.

* Smile – again, not too much and not at inappropriate times!

* Look interested. Don't keep looking away and fidgeting when they are talking.

* Plan topics to talk about in advance. If you've seen an amazing thing online or heard a weird story, store it in your mind until the right moment.

Social anxiety – sometimes called social phobia

Although it's quite natural to be shy and to find it difficult to talk to people, for a few people this is a huge problem that goes way beyond normal shyness. People who have a form of social anxiety (including selective mutism, where people sometimes find it impossible to get words out) may feel extreme stress and even panic when they have to interact with others. If this applies to you, there is help for you. Ask someone to support you to see a doctor, who can direct you towards treatment. You will also find online support groups for your age but seeing a doctor is still important.

Resources

SHYNESS AND SOCIAL ANXIETY

Social Anxiety UK: *www.social-anxiety.org.uk/*

Anxiety BC: *www.anxietybc.com/parenting/social-anxiety-disorder*

Moodjuice: *www.moodjuice.scot.nhs.uk/shynesssocialphobia.asp*

Value good friendship

Friendships can be among the best things in our lives but they can also be causes of huge upset and stress. Teenagers tend to rely on friends more than when they were younger. You may not want to talk to your parents about the things you used to talk about, so friends become even more important. Who you hang out with, and who 'accepts' you, becomes part of your identity, how you see yourself, and very much affects your self-esteem.

When friendships go wrong, or when you are finding it hard to fit in, it can feel like the worst thing in the world. Feeling excluded is a horrible experience which most people can identify with if they think about it. This can be deliberate or completely unintentional.

I've written a lot about friendships – the good and the bad – in *The Teenage Guide to Friends* and on my website. I offer you four of the most important tips here.

✳ 1. If your friendships are going wrong or if you're finding it difficult to make friends, see this as a temporary phase. Everything changes, especially at your stage of life. It's horrible now, but it will get better. There are more future friends for you out there. Try not to let it colour your opinion of yourself: it's just bad luck that you haven't found the people you gel with yet. Very often, the people around you are just wrapped up in their own problems, which can make them selfish. They are most likely not managing to put themselves in your shoes, as they just don't have the head-space.

✳ 2. There's no prize for having *lots* of friends. One or two good friends are all you need. Don't take any notice of the fact that some people seem to have loads of friends: too many friends can be a problem as you can't really maintain close or strong relationships with so many. Focus on one or two people you feel comfortable with; being relaxed with friends is really important and will allow you to make the most of the relationships as well as allowing you to show your best side.

✳ 3. Be good to your friends (but don't let them abuse your goodness). Show them you like them; thank them when they help you; share their happiness when something great happens to them; treat them just as you'd like them to treat you.

✳ 4. Be good to yourself. If someone doesn't make you feel comfortable, do they deserve to be your friend? Trusting people is good, but not if they keep walking over you. So, if there's someone who is supposed to be your friend but who you feel often manipulates you, always gets their own way, and seems always to think of themselves much more than you, consider whether it might be better to walk away gently from the friendship. They could be what we call a 'toxic' friend or a 'frenemy'. You don't have to stay with them if it's hurting you.

POSITIVELY YOU

A POSITIVE ATTITUDE

POSITIVELY HEALTHY

POSITIVELY BRAINY

POSITIVE ABOUT PEOPLE

A POSITIVE MOOD

Resources

VALUE GOOD FRIENDSHIPS

My Book, *The Teenage Guide to Friends*, has sections on making friends, keeping friends, and walking away if it's not working for you.

A reassuring resource for teenagers: *www.best-friends-forever.com/friend-issues.html*

From *Scientific American*, 'How to Deal with Frenemies': *www.scientificamerican.com/article/fickle-friends/*

Trust caring adults

Babies and young children – as with young animals of any sort – have to rely on the adults close to them, whose job it is to keep them safe, fed, warm and loved, and to teach them what they need to know. It's hard work being a new parent but it's also rewarding and exciting.

Most parents and carers do a great job, often helped by other relatives and supported by nursery workers and teachers who also care for the child. Some parents and carers struggle more than others, maybe through physical or mental illness or all sorts of pressures, so some children don't have the early support and love they need and deserve.

As you become a teenager, your relationship with the adults around you often changes, especially with the adults closest to you. Sometimes, you want to be more independent and do things for yourself. Or you may disagree with what some of the adults around you say or be *really* irritated by them! Being irritated by your parents or carers is very normal. Sometimes, you might have arguments and maybe say things you don't really mean and they might do the same.

There might also be times when you question whether you love your parents. Again, this is quite normal and natural. It can feel horrible at the time, but arguments and negative feelings do not mean that you or they are horrible people.

Relationships between parents and teenagers can be rocky for a while, but once you've gone through this period all is usually well. When you're feeling negative towards someone, try not to let that become bigger in your mind than necessary. Focus on being the best that you can and keep your mind on the things you can control.

Young children usually go to their parents or carers for help but you will probably want a range of adults to support you and you might prefer not to share a particular worry with your parents. That's OK. It's important to know who you can go to for help and reassurance. This is about knowing who your 'trusted adults' are. They can be different people for different situations. Sometimes, it might be your parents or carers. You might go to a teacher. Schools usually have a teacher who is assigned to student support or guidance; it might be your head of year, or a tutor, but there will be someone in the school whose job it is to help. But you can go to *any* teacher. Even if they don't know how to help with every situation themselves, they are trained in how to respond and how to help you get the right help.

Sometimes, you might prefer to talk to somebody who doesn't know you. That's when an organisation such as Childline becomes really important, as they are trained to know how to help you, whatever your problem.

Resources

TRUSTED ADULTS

Childline: *www.childline.org.uk/*

Your Life Your Voice has a page called 'Have a problem talking to your parents?': *www.yourlifeyourvoice.org/Pages/tip-problem-talking-to-your-parents.aspx*

Grow your empathy

Empathy is the ability to understand deeply what another person is feeling. We sometimes use the phrase 'walk a mile in someone else's shoes' to describe how we try to understand someone else. No one has perfect empathy but it's incredibly helpful if we can have as much as possible and it's important to try to develop it.

If we don't understand how the people around us are feeling, we might say the wrong things. If we do understand, we have a better idea of how to react. Empathy is one thing that helps us become effective humans, able to work well with others, but it also makes others behave better towards us. If we have strong empathy skills, we usually find it easier to make friends, especially if the people around us have good empathy skills, too.

How do we develop empathy?

Most humans start to develop empathy naturally between the ages of three and four. At that age we start to realise that what someone else feels or thinks might not be how we are feeling or thinking. This is called Theory of Mind, the idea that your mind is different from mine, that we may know, believe, think and feel different things. Then we gradually start to learn *how* particular events or situations make people feel and we can begin to guess what someone else might be feeling.

For example, we learn that if a pet dies, someone will be sad because they loved the pet. We learn that winning a prize usually makes someone feel fantastic, but that if they have to walk up onto the stage they might also feel embarrassed and shy or they might feel really proud, or a mixture. We learn that different people have different reactions.

How do we learn this? In two ways. First, by experiencing it ourselves, and second by listening to how people describe their feelings when they tell the story of their experience.

In fact, reading or hearing stories – true or made-up – are wonderful ways of growing empathy skills. Storytelling is something humans have done for many thousands of years, since long before written language. And many experts believe that the *reason* this habit and skill developed was because being able to understand how others think and feel is an incredibly powerful way to build connections, teams and groups. When we work together and share things, we can achieve so much more and empathy helps us work together. (Working on our own is also important, but if we do an amazing piece of work on our own and we have no one to share it with later, that wouldn't be so useful or satisfying.)

★ An empathy exercise

Think of someone you know who has quite a different life from you in some way. Maybe they have much more or less money, or a different family set-up, or any number of ways that you think they are different from you. Don't write their name down.

Write down one to three things that are different about their life compared to yours.

★ Write down one thing you think makes them luckier than you. Write down some things this might make them *feel*.

★ Write down one thing that makes them unluckier. Write down some things this might make them *feel*.

★ Imagine it is the person's birthday. What do they feel?

★ Imagine the person has just done badly in a test. What do they feel?

★ How do you feel when it's your birthday?

★ How do you feel when you've done badly in a test?

★ Are your feelings exactly the same as the other person's or not exactly? Why do you think that is?

You might have exactly the same feelings but you're more likely not to. If the other person has different things going on in their lives, their reactions and emotions will probably be a little different to yours. Not definitely, but probably. It's good to remember that. We can't be 100 per cent sure what someone else is feeling, but we can do our best to guess.

Resources

GROWING EMPATHY

EmpathyLab is a UK organisation focusing on the power of stories (true and made-up) to boost empathy. They work with schools in the UK – get your school to contact them: *www.empathylab.uk/*

EmpathyBomb, US organisation: *http://empathybomb.com*

Do things for others

Doing a good deed for someone else boosts our own mood and improves well-being. There's plenty of research about this. It gives us a warm feeling and raises self-esteem. It builds friendships. It also makes it more likely that the person will do something for us, though that isn't why we do it.

Doing things for others but never being thanked, or being ignored or taken for granted, does *not* make us feel better, of course. People should be grateful when another person helps them but if they are very upset, they might simply not have the headspace to recognise that someone helped them. That's understandable.

I'm not suggesting you do things for other people and never think of yourself. You have to think of yourself, too. But try doing some actions to help friends or people who need it, and you'll feel better. And the actions don't have to be big, either.

Ideas

✳ Hold the door open for an older person and smile at them

✳ Do a chore at home without being asked

✳ Give someone in your family a hug

✳ Offer to do small tasks for a neighbour who needs help: taking letters to post, weeding their garden, doing small bits of shopping

✳ Bake a cake for someone's birthday or to say thank you, sorry or good luck

✳ Make a home-made card for a friend.

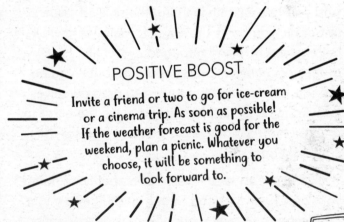

POSITIVE BOOST

Invite a friend or two to go for ice-cream or a cinema trip. As soon as possible! If the weather forecast is good for the weekend, plan a picnic. Whatever you choose, it will be something to look forward to.

Resources

DOING THINGS FOR OTHERS

Research into how doing a good deed for someone else boosts our mood and improves well-being: *sonjalyubomirsky.com/files/2012/09/Lyubomirsky-Layous-20132.pdf*

The Random Acts of Kindness website has lots of ideas and stories about this activity and its benefits: *www.randomactsofkindness.org*

A POSITIVE ATTITUDE

POSITIVELY HEALTHY

POSITIVELY BRAINY

POSITIVE ABOUT PEOPLE

A POSITIVE MOOD

Summing up

This section has revealed how the people around us make a difference to our lives and well-being. Building good relationships, both amongst your age group and the adults who care about you, will help your self-esteem and create a good network of people to have fun with, to share your life with and to support you when you need it. And you've seen that learning the skills of talking to people you don't know well is really worthwhile, helping you now and throughout your life. Face-to-face communication is important, but it can be difficult, so we sometimes need to drag ourselves away from our smartphones and make the effort to practise the skills of eye contact and face-to-face conversation.

You've learnt about the value of empathy, of doing your best to understand what someone else might be feeling. And remember how making someone else feel good helps make you feel good, too. Good relationships are about thinking both of what other people need and what we need ourselves, so try to ignore any negative people around you, people who drag you down, and focus on building relationships with positive people. And smile. There's a phrase, 'Smile and the world smiles with you'. I think it's a pretty good way of thinking.

A Positive Mood

Mood is different from well-being. Well-being, as you know, is about having generally good mental and physical health. Mood is about how you feel right now.

What kind of mood are you in at this moment? Start by thinking generally: good mood, bad mood or neither.

Then think in a bit more detail. Good, or positive, moods would usually make you feel any of these: happy, excited, proud, pleased, relaxed, comfortable, thrilled, content, alert. Negative moods would usually mean you feel any of these: worried, scared, sad, upset, shocked, devastated, undermined, low, numb, angry, disgusted, confused, stressed.

Sometimes we know why we're in a particular mood, but sometimes we don't. We can feel happy or sad without knowing why.

★ Analyse your mood

You might like to analyse your mood in more detail.

Get your notebook and write the date and the time of day.

★ Write whether your mood right now is positive, negative or neither.

★ Write as many words as you can think of to describe your feelings in more detail. You don't have to write sentences, just words that come to mind.

★ Write whether you know *why* you feel like that. Did something just happen to you or did someone say something? Did you just wake up feeling like this or did it happen during the day? Is this your usual mood or is it quite unusual?

★ You could do the same tomorrow or one day next week. See if there's any difference. Notice how things that people say or things that happen affect your mood.

Some things that affect mood are outside our control. I think it's helpful and positive to acknowledge those, so we don't spend time worrying about them. On the other hand, even if we can't stop them happening, we can sometimes take action to improve our mood anyway.

Here are some things we can't control:

✳ **Weather!** Usually, a warm or sunny day lifts people's moods. And a cold grey day does the opposite, especially if we have to go outside in it. A cold wind often makes me angry. Even though we obviously can't control the weather, we can stop it affecting us too negatively. We can find fun things to do indoors; we can make sure we wear warm enough clothes; we can do tasks we've been putting off for ages.

✳ **Hormones**. Hormones are chemicals that regulate all sorts of things, including appetite, sleep and growth. During adolescence, everyone experiences big increases in the hormones turning them into adults of whichever gender. These hormones can have a major effect on mood, making us feel sad or angry or easily irritated or excited. Many (but not all) girls notice this because of monthly cycles of hormones, whereas male hormones don't have monthly cycles so the differences are less obvious to them. But male and female hormones can be responsible for big mood swings. (If this affects you in a major way, a doctor will be able to give you good advice.)

✳ **Things that happen to us**. They might be big or small things but they will often affect our moods. It's just natural.

There are usually steps we can take to stop these factors affecting us too negatively or for too long. The ideas that follow will help you keep your mood as positive as possible. But don't worry if you sometimes feel down: it's completely normal and natural. It's part of being human. What we need are ways to keep those low feelings in their place: temporary and manageable.

Spot your signs of stress

Although stress isn't a 'mood', having too much stress can certainly lower mood. If we can spot signs of stress, we can use simple strategies to improve mood and well-being.

Stress is really important. Without it, we'd lie around all day and never push ourselves to super-perform! When there's any need to react to a difficult or dangerous situation, or any challenge, our brain triggers the chemicals adrenalin and cortisol to race around our body. This makes our hearts beat faster, pushing more blood (with oxygen and glucose) to where we need it: muscles of legs and arms, for example, to make us run faster or jump higher. And our 'nervous system' is also activated, helping us focus on the challenge and ignore irrelevant things.

This gives us the chance to super-perform. So, stress can be good!

The trouble is, we can have too much of it. There are two main problems:

★ Too much adrenalin can make us feel panicky. Then, instead of super-performing, we are likely to make mistakes or freeze.

★ Cortisol builds up in our system. Adrenalin disappears quite fast once the challenge is over, but cortisol hangs around. So, if you have more stress soon after, there's still cortisol from the earlier time. And after a time, the build-up can lead to major problems: difficulty sleeping; poor concentration and focus; being vulnerable to minor illnesses, such as colds; low mood; irritability. All of this adds up to lower well-being.

How do you know if you're suffering from too much stress? Not everyone reacts the same, but here are some common symptoms:

＊Lots of headaches or stomach aches

＊Often feeling dizzy or light-headed – this can also be from not eating enough food, so think about that first

＊Feeling sick

＊Appetite changes – this might be having little appetite or it might be feeling hungry all the time, but perhaps craving the wrong food

＊Poor sleep – you might find it hard to get to sleep or wake up often or early. Almost everyone experiences this sometimes, but if it's happening a lot, this is a possible sign of stress

＊Compulsive habits – biting nails, pulling hair, picking skin

＊Eczema

＊Feeling anxious without quite knowing why

＊Being snappy and irritable and finding it hard to control your temper or manage your anger.

Understand that these symptoms can be signs of something else, even though it's unlikely to be anything serious. If you experience any of them for more than a couple of weeks, see a doctor so that other illnesses can be ruled out. But they are very likely to be caused by stress.

Once you know how *you* react to stress, you can spot symptoms early and then take steps to prevent it getting worse. In that way, you'll have better control over your well-being and performance.

One important thing: being stressed is not a sign of weakness! It's completely natural, just like the symptoms of a cold or flu. Trying to ignore it is not the best way to have great well-being. My motto is: 'Know about it, notice it, nail it!'.

⭐ How I feel

Not everyone has the same signs of stress. This activity helps you begin to notice how it tends to affect *you* and *your* body. If you are feeling very relaxed and positive at the moment, you probably won't notice any of the symptoms in the list below – great! Instead, think of a time when you did feel worried, anxious or sad and see if you can remember how it made you feel. Then you can learn to spot the signs early and take steps to relax.

In your notebook, draw a picture of yourself. Your picture doesn't have to be brilliantly drawn: we just want to see where your head, arms and legs are!

Make a list of any of the following things you tend to notice when life is being difficult or worrying. Add any others you can think of. Shade in or highlight the parts of your body where you experience these things:

Frequent headaches

Unexplained stomach pains

Dizziness and feeling faint

Tight feeling in chest as though it's hard to take a full breath

Heart seems to be beating very fast

Feeling sick/nauseous

Jaw or face feels very tight

Muscles in neck, shoulders and jaw are tight

Biting fingers or chewing lip

Breathing feels high up in chest, not low down

Feeling panicky

Sweating a lot

Being extra clumsy

Not being able to concentrate

Sleeping badly

Twitching muscle near eye

Itchy skin or eczema.

These are all normal experiences and they don't do you any harm on their own, but they interfere with your enjoyment and can build up to make you too ill to work and achieve your best. By spotting the signs early and then following my advice in this chapter and the rest of the book, you can have the best possible control of your well-being.

POSITIVE BOOST

When you're feeling tense, notice whether your breathing seems high in your chest or lower down. Focus on shifting your breathing downwards so that your belly moves when you breathe, not your upper chest. Let your stomach muscles completely relax, flopping outwards. Notice how much more relaxed you feel, immediately. You'll find detailed instructions on the Internet if you search 'belly-breathing'. There's also a free audio on my website and **Resources** below.

Resources

SIGNS OF STRESS

My website has lots of advice, resources for schools, parents and teenagers. There is a lot of detailed advice in my book, *The Teenage Guide to Stress*, and I have classroom resources for schools to teach these important skills: www.nicolamorgan.com

From Kids Health: kidshealth.org/en/teens/stress.html

From Mind: www.mind.org.uk/information-support/tips-for-everyday-living/stress/signs-of-stress/

Manage your environment

Do you have a space that's your own? Your own bedroom would be perfect, of course, but if you share a bedroom you can still have an area that's yours, even just your bed and desk. Your space needs to work for you, no one else, so think about whether there's anything you'd like to change. Surroundings can make a big difference to mood and quite small changes can have major results.

Do you *like* your space? How does it make you feel when you're in it? Safe, comfortable, relaxed, happy? Or annoyed, uncomfortable, stressy, negative? Even if you love your space, you might get some ideas from the list that follows.

Ideas

Colours matter. Different colours can create different moods. For example, red and orange tend to make us feel excited or even anxious, rather than relaxed. Blue tends to be more relaxing, but of course there are lots of shades of blue (or anything else), from bright to soft, and dark to pale. It's really about what you like and what makes you feel the way you want. If you don't like the colour in your room, maybe you could help re-paint it? Maybe you could have a new duvet cover? Or put some things away and just keep the ones that are your chosen colours?

Messy room, messy mind? Actually, some people are genuinely fine about having a messy room, and maybe that's you (even if it isn't your parents!). But think carefully: do you feel more relaxed, in control and positive when your room is untidy or tidy? If you'd really like a tidy space, but have let the mess build up, it could be time for a big clean-up. You'll feel better.

Why not ask an adult for help? That might seem a really weird suggestion, but you could be surprised at how positively parents react if you ask in the right way. (Tip: you still have to do most of the work! You're just asking for help, not delegating the whole task.)

Place to work. Some people like to work at a desk while others prefer sitting on the floor. Have you got the best working space for yourself? Or you might have two spaces: a desk for writing and your bed or a cushion for reading. If you're working at a desk, you need a comfortable, adjustable chair, which doesn't have to be expensive. You need a good light in the right position so it doesn't make a shadow across your work. All this will help you feel better when you're working.

Some people notice a difference between working facing a wall, window or door. Experiment with what works for you. The next point picks up on this.

Feng shui. This was very fashionable about 20 years ago. Whole books were written about it. It is the art of arranging a room so that a positive energy is created. Even though it sounds odd, there are some good points. There are two things I think *can* make a difference: not having to step around items and not having a door behind us when we work.

You can test this for yourself: try putting your chair right in the path between the door and your bed and see how tense it makes you! And try positioning your desk so that you are sitting with your back to the door: you'll probably find it makes you nervous and alert, thinking that someone might come in without you noticing.

The main point is that it can make a difference where you put furniture. Be aware of this and experiment as much as you can. Aim to feel comfortable and secure.

Resources

EFFECTS OF COLOUR

Colour psychology, the possible effects of different colours:
www.verywell.com/color-psychology-2795824

Research on the colour red, particularly suggesting that red causes people to react with greater speed and force: *https://www.ncbi.nlm. nih.gov/pubmed/21500913*

Positive about music

Music can be a great way to affect your mood. If you want to be full of energy and raise your mood, choose faster, livelier music. If you want to relax and wind down, especially leading up to sleep time, choose slower, gentler music. Not everyone will have exactly the same reaction.

If you don't *like* the music, it probably won't have a positive effect on your mood. So, choose music that helps *you* achieve the mood you're looking for.

There are other relaxing sounds, too, such as birdsong or whalesong. You can find free audio recordings of these on the Internet.

Can you listen to music while you work?

Parents and teachers ask me this a lot and they usually believe you *shouldn't* work while listening to music. I understand why they think so. But I've looked into the science and thought carefully about this. Based on that, my answer is: if you want to and you find it helps you concentrate, it's usually fine to do it.

Here's why. In theory, listening to music does occupy some of your brain 'bandwidth' or thinking space. Everything does. So, in theory, that leaves a little bit less for concentrating on your work. But there are two reasons why listening to music can still be a good idea:

1. Some noises can be very irritating: noises of your family somewhere in the house, of a TV next door, of other students in your classroom making noises with their pens or feet, or sniffing. Sniffing is one of the *most* annoying things! And being irritated by something occupies a *lot* of brain bandwidth. So those noises can be terrible for concentration. Playing some music (when you're allowed to) blocks out those sounds and helps concentration.

2. You might have worries or thoughts buzzing around your head when you're trying to work. Playing music can then be helpful for getting 'into the zone'. Just as music can block out other sounds, it can also block out the 'noise' inside your head.

Choose your music carefully if you want to work well, though. It needs to be familiar to you, otherwise you'll be concentrating on the music too much. I play the same music over and over when I'm writing because I would never try new music if I want to concentrate. You *might* find it easier to concentrate if the music has no lyrics, as then you won't be listening to the words. But I find that doesn't affect me if I'm familiar with the music.

POSITIVE ABOUT MUSIC ←

However, some research suggests that tasks that involve memorising facts or lists do *not* benefit from music in the background.

One thing to be careful of: you can't listen to music during a test or exam. So, you don't want to get used to working with music. Make sure you sometimes work without. If people are annoying you with their noises in an exam or even in class, consider wearing ear-plugs. (But not when your teacher is talking to you!) I think ear-plugs are a great idea for exams.

Resources

BENEFITS OF LISTENING TO MUSIC

An article aimed at parents, on the benefit for teenagers of listening to music of their choice: *www.livestrong.com/article/515082-how-does-music-affect-teenagers-emotions/agers*

Mood changing music: *mamiverse.com/how-types-of-music-genres-affect-mood-64945/*

Music while you work – this article in the *Guardian* newspaper makes some useful points: *www.theguardian.com/education/2016/aug/20/does-music-really-help-you-concentrate*

Separating the tasks that may be positively affected and those that may be negatively affected: *www.qsleap.com/articles/listening-music-studying-good-bad/*

Does listening to music make you smarter? (Probably not.) *www.psychologytoday.com/blog/your-musical-self/201005/the-mozart-effect-doesnt-work*

A sense of sight

While we are thinking about mood, we should remember that what we see affects how we think and feel.

Sight is the most important and strongest sense for most humans, though, of course, people with impaired sight find other ways to experience the world and may have impressive other senses.

Here are a few things you might think about adding into your life to give you positive experiences through your eyes.

POSITIVELY YOU

A POSITIVE ATTITUDE

POSITIVELY HEALTHY

POSITIVELY BRAINY

POSITIVE ABOUT PEOPLE

A POSITIVE MOOD

A natural view

A great way to get a mood boost through your eyes comes from looking at nature – particularly green spaces and big spaces. There's a lot of research into the benefits of looking at a beautiful natural view. Scientists have discovered that hospital patients tend to heal more quickly if they can see beautiful scenery, even in a picture or mural. More research shows that being able to see green space outside your bedroom or house also improves mood.

But what if you live in a city? Go outside every day and make sure you see some natural scenery, whether the green space of a park, the sea or mountains in the distance. Every city has something to offer. Ask for a family trip at the weekend.

Research also suggests that we can have more creative ideas outside, or in a very high-ceilinged room, than indoors or under a low ceiling. So, get outside. Look at the sky, look at anything natural, and breathe the air!

POSITIVE BOOST

You don't have to be religious to be amazed by the brilliance of a cathedral, church, mosque or temple. The high ceilings, windows and statues are often incredible. Take a look and wonder at how people hundreds of years ago could have built them. The same applies to many ancient buildings. Just go and look: you'll be amazed.

Picture perfect

You can alter your mood by looking at different pictures. It's obvious really: looking at sad or frightening things will make us feel sad or frightened; looking at happy or fun things will lift our spirits. So, to feel more upbeat, find something that makes you feel happy to look at: a photo of a great holiday or something you did with your friends; a picture of kittens or puppies or baby lions or the sun or your sporting hero. Whatever makes you smile inside.

Resources

BENEFITS OF NATURE

Green spaces positively impact health and well-being, including for people in hospital: *www.forestry.gov.uk/pdf/fcpg019.pdf/$file/fcpg019.pdf*

Lots of benefits are mentioned here, with references: *greatergood.berkeley.edu/article/item/how_nature_makes_you_kinder_happier_more_creative*

The effects of living by the sea on well-being: *www.ecehh.org/research-projects/does-living-by-the-coast-improve-health-and-well-being/*

Natural environments help our attention span: *journals.sagepub.com/doi/pdf/10.1111/j.1467-9280.2008.02225.x*

Green spaces may improve children's learning: *http://www.pnas.org/content/112/26/7937.full*

Images of nature help people who are in pain: *www.clemson.edu/cafls/vincent/articles/effects_of_nature_images.pdf*

Sensible scents

Some people are not particularly affected by smell but for others it can be mood-changing. And it's quite easy to create something that has a smell you like. There are certain smells that make me go 'Mmmmmmmm' (yes, out loud). A few minutes before I wrote this my neighbour brought me a bunch of sweet peas from his garden and they are in my office right now – they are one of the best smells!

I use scented candles when I'm working or when I want to create a relaxed and warm mood at home. You might have something quite ordinary that you love the smell of – strawberries, banana, lemon, a particular soap, the smell of clean clothes, chocolate – and you could have it with you when you work. And often that *is* something you could take into an exam. Obviously, some things work better for that than others, but you can use your imagination and problem-solving skills to find a way to have your favourite smells with you when you want them. You might have a scented rubber or pen that you love, for example.

Laughter medicine

You might think you can only laugh if you're already in a good mood but, in fact, laughing can *put* you in a good mood! Obviously, you have to find something to make you laugh, but with YouTube and all the hilarious videos there, it should be fairly easy to find your favourites quickly. I love what appears when you search 'goats screaming like humans', 'dogs talking like humans' and 'babies eating lemons'. 'Babies laughing' also produces excellent results because laughter is catching: it's very hard to remain gloomy when babies are laughing.

But what's happening and why does laughter work so well? It turns out that the muscles we use for smiling and laughing trigger the brain into producing chemicals called endorphins, which people often call 'happy chemicals', because that's how they make us feel. They also take away pain.

Lots of people I know have particular comedy DVDs they will always watch when they need cheering up. It's a very good, simple way to give your mood a boost.

Resources

EFFECTS OF LAUGHTER

Laughing releases endorphins and affects social relationships:
rspb.royalsocietypublishing.org/content/279/1731/1161

Even smiling has positive effects: *www.psychologytoday.com/blog/
cutting-edge-leadership/201206/there-s-magic-in-your-smile*

Be engaged

Here's something interesting that can make a difference to your mood and so affect your well-being. Are you sometimes so involved in something that you don't notice the time? So 'into' a game or a book that you don't notice someone enter or leave the room, don't hear them talking to you, completely forget whatever else you're supposed to be doing?

This is called 'engagement' or being in 'flow'. And psychologists believe it's really important to our well-being to have enough periods like this.

Do you also know that feeling when you can't concentrate on what you're trying to do, can't get into a book, keep being distracted and delaying your work because you're just not interested enough in it? That's a very common and annoying state of mind – quite stressful, in fact. You want to get your work done or you want to switch off from your whirling thoughts but the tiniest things distract you. Every sound from people nearby seems loud and designed to irritate you. Even if the person near you isn't making a noise, you still *feel* their presence and you can't ignore them. This is the opposite of engagement.

So, how can we get into a state of engagement? There are many possible activities. I think they have to be things that need a lot of concentration, occupying a lot of what I like to call brain 'bandwidth'.

To understand this idea, think of computer or Internet capacity or speed and how, if something is occupying a lot of available 'bandwidth', other things happen more slowly. Our brains work quite like that: if something is occupying a significant amount of our mental processing capacity, there's less left over for other things and we work more slowly, less efficiently.

To get into a state of engagement, we need one of the activities that uses quite a lot of bandwidth, so we can be fully occupied in it. Here are some things I can think of that could work well. You might think of more. Remember that whatever it is, it has to be something *you* want to do and are interested in.

* Reading – anything you're interested in; fiction or non-fiction, short or long; graphic novels, too

* Investigating something on the Internet – again, it needs to be something you are really interested in

* Making something difficult – a complicated model, for example

* A puzzle – Sudoku or a difficult crossword

* A card game where you have to think hard

* Learning a poem by heart

* Learning to do something new

* Playing a musical instrument or singing

* Any physical activity you love and are trying to succeed in

* Watching your favourite sporting team

* A treasure hunt

* Drama

* Almost any hobby you really enjoy

* Something which gives you a goal or target

* Video or computer games (caution: these can be so engaging that you can be tempted to do them too much)

* Practising or making a speech

* Anything you find difficult but enjoyable

* Anything that needs concentration, but you are interested in the result

* Your school work, if it's something you're interested in

* Meditation.

You might wonder why I haven't included television. That's because generally it doesn't occupy much brain bandwidth. Sometimes it does, when it's a programme that grips you, but for most television not much effort is required. The point about engagement is that it requires some effort, some concentration.

It can be difficult to get into this state of engagement, so don't worry if you find it hard. Everyone struggles with this sometimes. But there are some ways we can help ourselves. When you want to concentrate on something, the three most important things are:

* Know what your goal is and why you're doing it. It could be that you want to read for half an hour for relaxation. Or it could be that you want to get your homework done quickly and well.

* Give yourself the best chance of not being disturbed. You might need to put a sign on your bedroom door or ask your parents for support.

* Remove the distraction of your phone or the Internet. If you must do something online, disable your social media accounts (see page 147).

POSITIVELY YOU

A POSITIVE ATTITUDE

POSITIVELY HEALTHY

POSITIVELY BRAINY

POSITIVE ABOUT PEOPLE

A POSITIVE MOOD

Don't worry about how many times you manage to feel engaged each day, as there's no rule. Just look for opportunities and notice how great it feels when you do get 'into the zone' and away from distractions of thoughts or external noises. (Do read **Just think** on page 196, because this will take the pressure off if you can't always concentrate.)

Resources

ENGAGEMENT

In Martin Seligman's PERMA model of well-being, E stands for Engagement. Here's an explanation: *www.thepositivepsychologypeople.com/perma-e-is-for-engagement/*

Here's Seligman talking about PERMA. He's speaking to psychology students, so younger listeners might find this a bit slow-going: *www.youtube.com/watch?v=iK6K_N2qe9Y*

Read for pleasure

Science shows masses of benefits from reading for pleasure. A daily or regular dose of a book you really enjoy can bring you better self-esteem, stronger empathy skills, more knowledge and vocabulary, better sleep, success at school, fewer problems with stress and generally better well-being.

So, if you love reading or if you liked it when you were younger but now feel you're too busy, or if you sometimes feel you should be working instead of reading for pleasure, take this as permission to do what you love: read! Curl up in a comfortable place, keep the other members of your household out: this is your time. And don't let anyone tell you this is time-wasting: tell them about the science that shows it's benefiting you, not wasting time.

I invented a word for this: readaxation. Readaxation means deliberately reading to relax. It works! You can try the activity on page 192, if you like.

★ A readaxation diary

First, read these statements and score 0–4 depending on how much you agree. Write the scores in your notebook. If you don't agree at all, score 0; if you strongly agree, score 4. Think carefully about your answers.

★ 'It is usually easy for me to find a book I'll enjoy.'

★ 'Ideally, I would like to read for pleasure every day if possible.'

★ 'It is easy for me to make time for reading.'

★ 'Often when I read, I get carried away and involved in the story.'

Now, each day for seven days, follow these steps:

★ Find a time when you won't be disturbed for about half an hour and a book you *want* to read. Find a comfortable place to read. (The best time is before bed.)

★ In your notebook, record your stress levels before you start reading, on a scale of 0–4. Think about symptoms such as: racing heart, shallow breathing, feeling anxious or tense.

★ Then read for about half an hour, letting yourself be carried away into the book.

★ Note your stress levels after you finish reading, again scoring 0–4.

If you didn't read on one day, DON'T record that day. Stop when you have seven days of records.

At the end of the week, ask yourself these questions:

★ Did reading an enjoyable book help me relax?

★ Do I think reading for pleasure might help lots of people feel better and be healthier?

★ Am I going to carry on doing it?!

(In **Resources** on page 195, you'll find a link to where you can download a readaxation diary. Your teacher or school librarian may well be interested.)

What should you read?

Whatever you want! Whatever you enjo
This is not a competition or an attempt to
'improve your mind' (though it will!). If you love fiction, read
fiction; if you prefer factual books, choose those; if graphic
novels are your taste, dive into them.

Sometimes an adult might comment that you've read that
book so many times and ask, 'Can't you choose a more
challenging one?' But this is reading for pleasure, not reading
for challenge and improvement. Sometimes you might want to
read a more 'challenging' book, but for now you want to read
this one. This is not the time for judgement. Adults don't like to
be judged on their reading choices, either.

Another thing adults might say is that a certain book is
'unsuitable' and might harm you. Very occasionally that might
be true, for example if you have a mental illness, such as
anorexia nervosa, anxiety disorder, or depression, reading
certain books might make you feel worse. If you have any of
these or similar conditions, do take advice on your reading
choices from your school librarian.

Sometimes adults want to protect teenagers from tough or
dark topics. This is quite understandable but it's my strong
opinion – and I'm not alone amongst reading experts in
thinking this – that for most young people, reading about dark
or frightening topics in a book aimed at their age group is the
safest place to explore these things. Better than the Internet,
where there is no control over the content. Stories (true and
made up) are great ways to process worries and grow our
resilience and empathy.

If a book is going to be too dark for you, you will probably
know this before anything bad has happened and you'll be
able to put the book down. People do that all the time. I do.
So, read what interests you and be alert to how it affects
your mood.

Why is reading for pleasure so good?

There are two main reasons. First, it occupies many areas of
the brain and requires concentration, so it is easy to 'engage'
deeply. Second, it allows us to forget our worries for a while.
After all, you can't be fully involved in a book *and* worry at the
same time.

What if you don't like reading?

That's OK. Not everyone does. And if you don't like it, I won't
force you. But there are so many benefits that I'd love you to
know them and see whether you'd like to try again. Remember:
you can read *anything*, either in print or on an e-book reader.
It can be true or made-up; it can be about sport, heroes,
crocodiles, baking, murderers, highwaymen, horses, cars; set in
India or Iceland, the desert or underwater; featuring characters
of every colour or background, from history or today; sad or
happy or funny or scary. You can have as many pictures in it as
you want. It's your choice.

What about audio books?

Excellent idea! Of course, it's not doing exactly the same thing
in your brain (because any two different activities will have
some different effects) but it's a very valid way of relaxing and
of engaging in a book and its characters, events and emotions.
So, if you like listening instead of reading yourself, go for it.
Lots of adults like this, too.

When should you do it?

Whenever you feel like it! I think the best time is before bed,
after you've done everything to get yourself ready for sleep.

Most people find this is a great way to switch off the day and will find themselves feeling sleepy quite quickly. Some people find they get so excited by the book that they can't feel sleepy, especially if the book is really exciting. If this happens to you, it's best to set a timer and don't read for more than about 45 minutes.

POSITIVE BOOST

Can you remember a story you loved when you were much younger? Could you find it now? Maybe you have younger siblings and love their books? Go and find one you love. Have fun reading it. Remember how you felt as a child. Just take five minutes with one of these lovely, inspiring books.

Resources

READING FOR PLEASURE

Science shows masses of benefits of reading for pleasure. The 2015 UK Reading Agency report gathered the research: *readingagency.org. uk/news/media/reading-for-pleasure-builds-empathy-and-improves-well-being-research-from-the-reading-agency-finds.html*

My website has lots of links to research and resources, including a readaxation diary to monitor the stress-relieving effects of reading before bed. Go to *www.nicolamorgan.com* and see the Reading Brain section or put "readaxation" into the search box.

Just think

It's something many people don't do much anymore: just spending time thinking. Any bits of spare time we have, we seem to fill with entertainment, or connecting with other people online or getting information or messages from our phones or other devices. All those things are *good* but because so many of us (including me!) have a phone with us pretty much all the time, it's so easy just to pick up that device instead of spending time in our own heads.

Why might that matter? What's the problem if your mind and time are filled with all that lovely online activity and there's no time to think freely? (This applies to all age groups, by the way, even though I'm saying 'your'.)

I think it matters for several reasons.

* It's mentally exhausting. All these activities use brain energy. Just as you have to rest your body sometimes, you also have to rest your brain. Otherwise it won't work so well.

* The messages on smartphones or computers are often stressful. If you haven't got enough 'likes' on a post or if someone else's selfie looks so much more gorgeous than yours or someone says something slightly (or very) undermining, it will dampen your mood. If that happens too much, it's not healthy.

* Thinking is important and creative and exciting!

Let's consider that last one. Creative people say that their best ideas don't usually come when they're staring at a computer screen but when they're walking, or on a bus or train, or in the shower or bath or doing nothing much. Ask any writer, artist, engineer, designer or computer game creator.

And it's not just people who obviously need creative thinking time. It applies to people who start businesses, planning how to make their dreams come true. Teachers, thinking about a problem with a class. Film-makers, constructing their next project. Parents, wondering how to help their children feel more confident at school or how to plan a weekend activity for everyone to enjoy. Scientists and psychologists, grappling with a new idea. Gardeners, deciding when to sow seeds for the best crop. Managers, working out how to make their staff function better.

It's not just for work, either. We all need time to think about ourselves, our dreams, problems, strengths, ideas. What we want from life and how to get it, our friends, how to help a friend in need and how to thank a friend for something they've done.

There's even research to suggest that deliberate daydreaming time helps creative thinking and forward-planning. Scientists believe that it's when we're *not* actively thinking about something that our mind can be doing its best work. I'm not saying you can spend all day daydreaming, especially in class, though! This research is about *deliberately* letting your thoughts drift every now and then, not letting anyone else (or a smartphone) distract you, but letting your mind wander for a while. Then come back to the task and you could find that your thinking is better. This is particularly useful when you've been struggling with something you're trying to understand or work out: if you spend maybe 20 minutes of real effort and then go for a short walk to the shops or lie in the garden for a while, or on your bed, maybe listening to music but not focusing on anything in particular, you'll often find that when you go back to what you struggled with, you can do it. Our minds do a lot of work when we aren't trying! But we have to give ourselves mental space for that to happen.

The world needs thinkers and thinkers need thinking time!

Ideas

* Next time you're on any transport, leave your phone hidden away. Just don't take it out. Look out of the window and let your mind freewheel.

* Is there something you want to think about or need to plan? A school project or play, something you want to do with your friends? Set some time aside for it. Put your phone away and switch the Internet off.

* Go for a walk on your own. (Be safe.) Focus on what you can see and hear around you.

* Have a bath, with no book, magazine or phone to occupy you.

* If you find it difficult or even scary just letting your mind freewheel, try some simple meditation or mindfulness techniques. Try the relaxation technique on page 199.

* Help settle your mind with a simple activity that doesn't require much thought: weeding the garden, colouring in,

knitting (if you're quite good at it), using a stress ball, making a collage of bits cut from magazines, listening to music. All these things take up a little bit of brain bandwidth, but not too much. You can still think while doing them.

This kind of thinking time really can't be done with anyone else so it's especially important for quieter or introverted people, who need time on their own. Kind people might come and ask if you're OK, so just say: 'Definitely, but I'm thinking and I need peace and quiet for that.'

Don't be afraid of 'doing nothing'. It's really good for you (sometimes)!

POSITIVE BOOST

Sit or lie somewhere really comfortable, where you won't be disturbed. Breathe in deeply through your nose and out more slowly through your mouth. Close your eyes. Focus on your toes and feet. Tense those muscles, and then relax. Now move to your legs and do the same. Do this tensing and relaxing for each part of your body, working your way up to your head.

Think of the tension floating away through the top of your head. Think about each muscle in your face and jaw. Continue breathing in a relaxed way. Feel your muscles get heavier and softer. Stay like this for as long as you want. When you're ready, open your eyes and get up slowly.

Resources

THINKING

Freedom to Think: *http://freedomtothinksite.tumblr.com/about*

Deliberate daydreaming may help creative thinking and forward-planning: *www.telegraph.co.uk/news/2016/05/23/daydreaming-can-boost-your-daily-productivity--research-suggests/*

The *Atlantic*, with references to various studies into the need for young people to have daydreaming and thinking time: *www.theatlantic.com/education/archive/2013/10/teach-kids-to-daydream/280615/*

Some successful people and their attitude to thinking time: *www.inc.com/empact/why-successful-people-spend-10-hours-a-week-just-thinking.html* (Aimed at adults, but these same things should apply to you.)

POSITIVE BOOST

What would you like as a reward for learning so much? Half an hour lying in the park? A cinema trip with friends? A day at the beach? Cake or ice-cream, just for a treat? Whatever it is, as long as you're allowed, go for it. You deserve it!

Focus on the positive

This book is all about focusing on the positives and this section is about having a positive mood, but sometimes bad things happen, even when we do everything right.

When that happens, it's completely natural to feel really negative, whether sad, shocked, angry, scared, guilty, regretful, confused or whatever. But after a while we have to start to pick ourselves up. That's when tricks to focus on the positives come in useful.

Sometimes, nothing in particular has happened, but we still feel a bit low. It's often too easy to think about the bad stuff when in fact there are loads of good things in our lives.

POSITIVELY YOU

A POSITIVE ATTITUDE

POSITIVELY HEALTHY

POSITIVELY BRAINY

POSITIVE ABOUT PEOPLE

A POSITIVE MOOD

When something difficult happens, we can't control how we feel about it straightaway, because emotions just happen, rather than being things we decide. A bit later, however, we *can* begin to control how we feel. In fact, that's part of well-being: being able to decide that we're going to feel better and taking steps to make that likely. Sometimes we might need a bit of extra help and that's when it's sensible to see a doctor. Also, of course, really major bad things take longer to recover from.

But for most people, most of the time, there are things we can do to help us focus on positives rather than negatives.

Ideas

✱ Make sure you have something to look forward to. What is it? A holiday? Birthday? Christmas? What do you hope it will be like? Or something closer in time: fix up a trip to the cinema; arrange to meet a good friend. Something nice at the weekend can make the whole week feel better.

✱ What went well? Don't forget to say what character strengths you used.

✱ Positive daydreaming. You can be as creative as you like and no one will ever know what you're daydreaming about. It could have all your heroes in it; you could have loads of money and be thinking about how to spend it; you could win prizes and achieve your heart's desire. Or you could be lying on a perfect beach, at peace, with just the sound of lapping waves. It's just a story and you can control it.

✱ In your notebook, jot down: three good things about your life; three goals you have for next week; three people who are on your side; three positive things about being teenage.

Summing up

You might have thought mood was something you can't control, that you just wake up in a good or bad mood. Certainly, outside events affect mood and sometimes it's not easy to be happy when difficult thoughts are spinning around.

But I hope you see now that there are quite simple things you can do to improve your mood. This section has given you a whole load of practical suggestions to help you manage your well-being, beginning with knowing how to identify your own stress symptoms, and then using your environment, music, laughter, engaging hobbies, reading or just thinking and daydreaming for a while to give yourself a break from our busy world.

Mood is a bit like a snowball: roll it and it gets bigger. So make sure you roll with your good moods, adding positive things to them, and trample on your bad moods so they don't have a chance to snowball.

★ The FLOURISH test again

Remember you did the FLOURISH test near the start of the book? How about doing it again, as long as you haven't read the whole book in the same day?! If you have, do it again this time tomorrow. Did you score better the second time?

Finally...

So, there you have it: everything I can think of to keep you positively teenage!

You might have started this book because you were excited about being a teenager or just plain curious about what might lie ahead. Being curious is a really good reason to read a book like this because information and understanding are so empowering. Or you might have had some worries and been looking for reassurance – I certainly hope *Positively Teenage* is full of it. You might already have started noticing that your thoughts and feelings weren't behaving quite the same as they did a couple of years ago and you wanted to know how normal that is. Answer: very!

I hope the main thing you've discovered is that you can control far, far more than you thought. You've learnt loads of strategies to use throughout your life, starting with these exciting, dramatic, changing teenage years. If things go wrong, you can be resilient, pick yourself up, grow stronger and move forward. You have a huge toolbox to control physical and mental well-being and be positive about your life, your potential, yourself. Many of the tools adults should know but often don't: maybe you can share all this knowledge with parents and teachers.

You have the power to make yourself FLOURISH, throughout your life. Use your powers well!

Be truly, positively teenage!

Glossary

Adolescence – literally 'becoming adult'; the stage of development between child and adult.

Adrenalin – (also 'adrenaline') a chemical (**hormone**) produced in the body to make us super-alert, strong and ready for action, especially when we are scared or excited.

Aerobic exercise – also called 'cardio', this is light to moderate exercise that we can keep going for some time, unlike sprinting or weight-lifting that we can only do briefly.

Body Mass Index – a healthy weight must relate to our *height, age and sex*. A BMI chart shows the healthy range for each of us.

Calories – usually given as kcal or kilocalories, measurements of the energy that a particular portion of food would provide. If we don't eat enough calories, we lack energy, our brain works less well and we may be unhealthily thin.

Cortisol – along with adrenalin, a **hormone** the body produces in response to stress, making us alert and ready for action in the face of threat or need to perform super-well.

Diabetes – there are two main types of diabetes, involving failure to produce or process insulin, which regulates blood sugar or **glucose**. In Type 1, which usually begins in childhood, patients need daily injections and must monitor blood sugar very carefully. Type 2 is much more common and is diet-related. It is usually managed through diet and weight. Diabetes is a growing problem in countries where people eat too much sugar.

Diuretic – anything which makes the body produce more urine.

Dopamine – an extremely important brain chemical (neurotransmitter) which helps **neurons** send messages around the body. It's vital for learning and memory, mood, pleasure and excitement, sleep, and many other human behaviours.

Eczema – a condition where patches of skin become extremely dry and itchy. It can be helped with creams and by avoiding things that trigger it, which differ between sufferers.

Endorphins – **hormones** produced in the brain which make us feel less pain.

Genes – the bits of 'code' that we inherit from our biological parents and that affect many aspects of how we look, grow and behave. Genes are 'switched on or off' by the environment or things that happen to us, too, so it's more complicated than simply inheriting them. Genes are not responsible for *everything* about us but they are fascinating and important.

Glucose – a simple sugar which our body processes, using the **hormone** insulin, and carries in the blood to use as energy. People with **diabetes** have to test the glucose level in their blood.

Heart rate – how many times the heart beats per minute. When we are sitting still and feeling calm, our heart beats more slowly than when exercising or stressed. People who are very fit tend to have a slower 'resting heart rate' than others. Healthy heart rate varies according to age.

Hormones – chemicals produced in the body which regulate everything our bodies do. The sex hormones, for example – testosterone, androstenedione, oestrogen and progesterone – make the bodily changes that turn us into a fully developed adult of whichever sex. There are hormones to control appetite, sleep, growth, mood, digestion and every process our body needs to be healthy. There's even one – oxytocin – that makes you feel love or desire!

Neuron – also called 'nerve cell', cells in the brain and spinal cord which send messages to the rest of the body. We are born with around 100 billion neurons and later we lose many of these as part of natural, healthy pruning. We don't need them all! Our skills and abilities come from how well our neurons connect into pathways, not how many neurons we have. Every time we practise anything, we grow and strengthen these pathways.

Nutrients – all the parts of food that help nourish us, including vitamins, proteins, minerals. Each nutrient has a special job so it's important to eat a wide range of foods. The word 'nutritious' comes from the same word.

Prefrontal cortex – the area of the brain at the very front, more developed in humans than other animals. It's often called the 'control centre' because we use it for things such as controlling actions and thoughts, making good decisions, working things out, making moral judgements, understanding what might happen next. It's the last area of the brain to develop fully, which happens well into our 20s.

Puberty – the stage when 'secondary sex characteristics' begin to develop, with the biological function of making us able to reproduce. Young people (usually from about age 10/11 for girls and 12 for boys, though this varies a *lot* between individuals) will notice many changes in their bodies, with some starting earlier or later than others. Puberty is triggered by the sex **hormones**.

Psychology – the study of behaviour, why we do and feel the way we do. Early psychologists studied what went wrong and how to fix it but psychology now also focuses on how to prevent problems by understanding how we all work.

Social anxiety – anxiety in social situations is very common and most people feel a bit nervous or shy when they are with people they don't know well. But social anxiety (also called social anxiety or social phobia) is a more extreme form of this, where a sufferer finds it really difficult or impossible to cope in social situations and becomes extremely stressed. There is better understanding of this now and lots of help available.

Species – in biology, a species is a group of animals similar enough to breed naturally together. Humans and gorillas are both 'primates' (apes) but they are not the same species. The species name for humans is *Homo sapiens*. Barn owls and snowy owls are both owls but they are each a different species of owl; they don't breed together.

Index